WESTERN SADNESS

THE PSYCHOPATHOLOGY OF MODERNITY

ASHLEY DYMOND

Copyright © Ashley Dymond, 2021

All Rights Reserved

This book is dedicated to Jen Dymond,
the bravest person that I have ever known.

Contents

Chapter 1: Introduction 1

Chapter 2: Technology 5

Chapter 3: Icons 14

Chapter 4: Entertainment 28

Chapter 5: Mass Media 38

Chapter 6: Social Media 48

Chapter 7: Materialism 60

Chapter 8: Socialisation 65

Chapter 9: Occupation 75

Chapter 10: Liberty 82

Chapter 11: Social Order 90

Chapter 12: Social Divisions 106

Chapter 13: Criminal Justice 123

Chapter 14: Healthcare 134

Chapter 15: Individuality (Pt. A) 145

Chapter 16: Individuality (Pt. B) 160

Chapter 17: Friendship 176

Chapter 18: Abuse 182

Chapter 19: Virtue 190

Chapter 20: Conclusion 195

Chapter One: Introduction

Who?

At the time of publishing, this book was written by a twenty-two-year-old psychology BSc (Hons) student at the University of Derby. In other words, a young man without any formal qualifications in anything remotely sociological or psychological wrote 50,000+ words about psychopathology in modern Western society. Resultantly, it would be irresponsible of Mr. Dymond (who is referring to himself in the third person for the sake of syntactic consistency) to write a book to advise readers on topics surrounding self-improvement or anything else whereby the author directly attempts to improve the quality of life in the reader. Therefore, Ashley has written an opinion piece on why he feels that the West is not the 'best' in relation to how its social order affects the emotional welfare of its citizenry, rather than a self-help book where he would inevitably risk misinforming the reader and put them at risk.

Below is an excerpt from Ashley Dymond's blog 'Curious Collywobbles' where he somewhat sarcastically describes himself to his readers:

"By day, Ashley Dymond is an award-winning line manager and training instructor working in the noble sector of health and social care, as well as a psychology student at the University of Derby. By night, Ashley Dymond comes before you as but a 'humble' writer, utilising his limitless academic and vocational knowledge of social... stuff... for the grand benefit of all who aspire to comprehend the exasperating enigmas of mental health."

What?

The book will describe specific mental health issues and propose their most likely causes, chapter by chapter. For example, it may describe the symptoms of various forms of psychosis, evaluate the most likely reasons for the extent of their development, and query why broken families have more schizophrenic children. All in all, Ashley's primary concern is to inform the reader on how the most 'common' mental health issues develop and why they do.

When?

This book is written as a critique of today's world; it is not the author's interest to write about historical events, at least where they pose little to no relevance. Instead, it describes how contemporary cultures influence people's emotions before evaluating the positive and negative effects on human emotional welfare.

Where?

As the title states, the author's analysis of mental health is localised in modern Western society. The 'West' refers to more economically developed countries such as the USA, Australia, and the majority of Europe. Within these countries, diagnosing mental illnesses is becoming increasingly common, unlike in the rest of the world, where physiological needs are the primary concern. Thus, with this book, Ashley aims to explain to the reader why Western cultures cause such a massive level of unhappiness among their citizenry.

Why?

To identify what has changed in society to cause such a rise in divorce rates, mental health diagnoses, and suicide, among other calamities. The stoic mentality of previous generations has been forgotten; life is now too emotionally demanding. As a result, today, Westerners are more depressed and insecure now than ever before. Why is this?

Additionally, it is vital to quickly state that it is the author's well-researched and informed opinion that both genetic and environmental influences cause mental illnesses, whether it be a combination of one's chemical imbalances in their brain and how they were emotionally abused as a child or a variety of two other things. Therefore, both nature and nurture influence people's well-being, although there is a debate to be explored across this text as to how dominant each of these factors is in determining human emotion. Ultimately, this book aims to look beyond the mere individual power of DNA, neurotransmission, or the immediate environment. Instead, this book seeks to examine how all these factors interlink.

How?

Through providing readers with informed opinions on psychopathology in modern Western society, which is also valuable enough to help them understand the deep-rooted origins of mental health issues, which they might also learn to talk to others about their problems and even to reverse their symptoms by making more informed decisions on how to improve their well-being after considering a wide range of possible psychopathological causes. However, it is not the aim of the book to replace or undermine the usefulness of professional psychological aid, which will always be the safest and most reliable solution in relation to overcoming mental health issues.

Chapter Two: Technology

What is technology?

Inside Western culture today, technology is generally viewed as a material category encompassing the electrical machinery that characterises the daily happenings in First World societies. Crucially, the Western man is dependent on electrical machinery to complete his essential activities such as communication, leisure, and navigation. Without integral modern-day technologies like mobile phones, today's revelations would remain but the ambitious dreams of yesterday. However, of course, the word technology does not simply refer to electrical mechanisms. The word's semantics prove rather vague; 'technology' can stand for anything that performs a technical function of design. Naturally, this raises issues when describing and evaluating the sociological and psychological effects of technological creation and utilisation across the West.

Technology, according to this text, is both a godsend and a curse. Throughout history, artificial mechanisms have allowed for the positive development of individual and societal welfare through revolutionary inventions in medicine and transport. Nevertheless, conversely, they have also catalysed cultural regression via the heedless production of cataclysmic arsenals of warfare that could still one day prove to be the end of humanity itself.

Industrialisation

Between the eighteenth and nineteenth centuries, Europe and the United States embarked on a socioeconomic transition as new technological advancements inspired by the enlightenment altered the means of material production; this is known as the industrial revolution. Ingeniously, the invention of the steam engine powered factories, threshing equipment, and trains were born from the industrial revolution. The inventive use of the farming equipment meant fewer agricultural workers were required to harvest farmland crops, and prospective employees had to look to the rapidly expanding industrial cities for employment. Within these goliath conurbations, colossal factories were built to significantly accelerate the production rates of various material goods such as cotton in mill factories like Strutt's North Mill located in Belper, Derbyshire. Remarkably, the construction of these factories might be regarded as the most important contributing factor to the urbanisation of the West, which infamous German Karl Marx historically cites as the death of the material stage of feudalism, thus the dawn of capitalism.

According to Marxists, the socioeconomic shift caused by industrialisation pivoted many cultural changes to the superstructures of a new capitalist society. Previously, peasant children would learn agriculture from their parents and community at home. However, now the education system was open to socialising a submission to authority that mirrored the industrial workplace where the patriarchal heads of working-class households would be exploited as low-wage machine operators by their bosses, characterising the renewed dialectical materialism composed of the oppressed proletariat and the dominant bourgeoisie.

The industrial revolution reportedly led to many forms of economic oppression. For example, workers were alienated from their products as they did not own them like the peasants 'owned' their crops. Additionally, workers were exploited for their cheap labour, which Marxists claim that they had no choice to perform as it was the only marketable thing that they had of value to retain a barely durable quality of life. Finally, primarily due to technology, capitalism also formed a new societal base that governments built superstructures upon, like industrial workplaces that further oppress its citizenry.

The ideology of capitalism promotes individualism as people were fed the delusion that anybody could become rich as with workplace dedication came lucrative rewards in the free market. Nevertheless, observably, much of the managerial and professional figures in any workplace already hailed from affluent families who could spend more money on private education, inherited material wealth, and most importantly, lived in a culture tailored to suit their benefits.

French sociologist Emile Durkheim famously wrote that the conflict-inducing and manipulative aspects of capitalism drove much of the workforce to suicide; endless hordes of ruthless competition fiercely combated for the few wealthy occupational positions that remained illusively unobtainable nonetheless. Sadly, the myth of social mobility might still be perpetuating the modern West's dysfunctional capitalism due to the prominence of social issues like poverty. However, some claim that more recent technological inventions have wholly eradicated the inequalities of economic conflict and paved the way for a new era, postmodernity.

Postmodernism

Aptly named postmodernists, the advocates of postmodernism suggest that inventions becoming widely accessible in the twentieth century lifted the metaphysical barriers of space and time across society: telephones allowed for people living over long distances to communicate in an instant, automobiles enabled quickened travel, television provided access to entertainment shows from the comfort of the home, and later the internet gifted everyone with the ultimate all-access package. Furthermore, new work and lifestyles arose after technological developments and their subsequent cultural alteration of shared values. For example, in the workplace, skills were more widely accessible in and outside the education system with the demand for more engineers and technicians and the creation of the internet. Culturally, since social class naturally became irrelevant in a society that cannot demand extortionate prices for standard technologies, nobody cares about cultural signs of wealth or the collection of material content anymore. Instead, societal values are placed on an expression of individual identity through outward appearance. Therefore the price tag of a product means a lot less to the average person than the image of the product itself or the ethical message it sends.

Although brands are associated with particular images that they can charge more money for, and the expense of consumption of exclusively 'cruelty-free' produce has controversially proven to be expensive. Therefore, whether it be wearing clothing made by an expensive brand or adopting a morally superior lifestyle, outward appearance often remains an indicator of privilege and postmodernists are ignorantly optimistic of the effects modern technologies have made on social class. These technological developments may psychologically worsen the lives of the economically deprived as simultaneously forced to engage in less 'politically correct' lifestyles and shamed for their supposed inconsideration.

Communication

Mobile phones, electronic mailing systems, and social media outlets have utterly reformed the methods by which people communicate information with each other. Presently, using technology to send a picture to a friend or a message to a potential date are examples of the primary mode of informally socialising, whilst emails and phone calls dominate the communicatory measures of growing business connections, negotiation, and other formal proceedings. Notably, these normalised behaviours are convenient so as to avoid the trouble of physically travelling from one place to another to deliver these communications. Also, society enforces them with the introduction of short, mandatory response deadlines. The lack of physically social activity theoretically matches growing complaints of social anxiety in many young people today, so it is not unreasonable to allege that technology is increasingly hindering the emotional welfare of people in the West and perhaps even globally.

Irresponsibly, the negligibly relaxed regulation on social media platforms of cyberbullying and online discrimination allows abusers to escape punishment via anonymity and provides them with no incentive to stop. Therefore, this untapped need for personal identification when creating social media accounts inspires malicious individuals to ceaselessly abuse anyone they wish to, typically derailing their self-esteem and scaring them. Of course, social media platforms do at least have codes of conduct users must adhere to, on top of enabling users to 'block' any other users that they do not wish to hear from. Still, the surviving ability for users to create new accounts without reason eternalises their tendency to bully, discriminate, and threaten whomever they feel like, whenever they feel like it.

Addiction and Overstimulation

The recreational use of technology has proven to sell marvellously well. Mobile apps, social media platforms, and video game consoles are prime examples of the immense success of leisurely technologies for providing a multitude of happy neurotransmission. The continuous, chemical hits of dopamine grow to be such a commonplace stimulation that when a person goes too long without them, they can suffer a form of withdrawal... because they are addicted due to their overstimulation.

The cognitive longing for a biochemical reaction proves to be such an overpowering distraction from people's daily schedules that it becomes a part of it. Moreover, the urge to check their phone or stay online that moment longer can significantly disrupt and harm that individual's sleeping cycle. In extreme cases, this subjective form of self-harm can even develop into insomnia. Elsewhere, the overconsumption endured by rapidly jumping from genres of information from short videos online would surely lower the attention spans of consumers and make it more difficult for them to focus their attention on more productive tasks, perhaps even leading to further medical diagnoses of illnesses such as attention deficit hyperactivity disorder (ADHD) and clinical depression because of difficulties individuals experience when attempting to focus or consider their lowered self-esteem, respectively. Apart from acknowledging low productivity levels, self-esteem issues also appear when analysing the fact that many social media users deem the quantity of 'likes' that their picture receives as a measurement of their validity, most notably in relation to their physical beauty. Thus, a person who obtains only four likes is more likely to show mood disorders like clinical depression than their friend who hypothetically obtained eighty. It is possible to have too much of a good thing.

Power Generation and Weaponry

Technology of all kinds holds grand influence over the culture of society; the designed purposes of machines encourage fundamental standards of behaviour required for a person to activate the function of a specific technology. For example, the designed use of hunting rifles depends on a person's maliciousness to kill another living creature. Thus the mere existence of hunting rifles encourages this form of behaviour in the societies in which they exist. Furthermore, nuclear weaponry with the ultimate potential to destroy entire civilisations left to the disposal of the few world leaders sets an astoundingly violent example to the rest of humanity. It collaterally lowers the globally shared value of human life itself as our species survival (among other things) is detrimentally dependent on one crazed, irresponsible dictator taking the immensely destructive plunge and kicking off the shortest world war of all time. It is difficult for human beings to love one another when we are our own most significant threat.

Aside from dictatorial and nuclear power, pollution also stands among the largest social issues in the West, and it is all technologies fault. The technological overuse of fossil fuels has proven that the Western authorities are incapable of considering the welfare of future generations as they consistently fall victim to their selfish individualism. Not only have these democracies starved the future of fuel, but they have released an unholy amount of greenhouse gas into the Earth's atmosphere and endangered everyone with the treacherous hazard of climate change. Honestly, the majority of Western leaders do not care about obvious global dangers such as...: wildfires, rising seas levels, heatwaves, wildlife extinction, and intense drought, all because it can put a pretty penny in their bottomless pockets. Therefore, the

West hereby declares to "take what you wish and serve only yourself!"

What does the future hold?

As Europe and North America become more and more computerised, the general levels of occupational security deplete rapidly. Some factories no longer need to employ manufacturing workers when they can invest in autonomous machines, switchboard operators can kiss their financial stability goodbye thanks to telephonic technology rendering them obsolete, and sales assistants have been left feeling anxious next to their new robotic competitors at the self-service kiosks. Naturally, skilled technicians and engineers are likely to benefit from the upcoming renewed age of electricity as extra machinery means extra opportunities for them. However, years down the line, new independent creative artificial intelligence (AI) will not steal their beloved jobs too. Whatever the case may be, the types of available future work are protectively limiting, and people will not follow their dreams. That is unless humans finally decide that liberty is more important to their emotional wellbeing than scientific 'advancement'.

Client-centred therapy is inherently distinguished by an empathetic approach on behalf of one human being to another. Considering the sheer complexity of the human mind, the belief that AI will possess the ability to mirror this for many decades, or perhaps centuries to come, is asinine. However, according to many overzealous neuroscientists and other puppeteering authority mouthpieces, the arrival of an impressive technological feat in AI psychiatry is imminent. Hopefully, these are empty promises or misguided delusions because endeavouring to use mechanical constructions for the necessary provision of intrinsically qualitative mental health support is set up to fail.

Maybe humanity should fear an uprising of artificial intelligence, perhaps not for the cliched sake of rebellious robotic warriors, but more so of a fundamentally generalising guessing game senselessly trying to mimic humanistic compassion that distinguishes empathic therapy. If operated irresponsibly, both history and logic indicate that therapeutic AI could genuinely be the death of humanism…

Chapter Three: Icons

About an Icon

Postmodernists argue that the technological revelations of modernity have catalysed a societal transition of shared values and norms via a metaphysical erosion of social barriers in space and time. Whilst the phenomenon of postmodernity remains controversial, a compelling yet damning postmodernist's take is unveiled through analysis of this expression when evaluating the cognitive impacts of influential personalities through social media. The enlarging quantity of influential personalities (icons) correlates with the ascending significance of social media in society. Perhaps this is because social media serves as a universal platform for any icon to establish themselves, expand their brand, or spotlight other potential icons. If so, this would mean that the growth of social media usage has caused the growth of iconic figures seen in society.

Still, what is an icon? The word "icon" can be attributed to anyone known to enough people to hold a significant degree of influence. Since the semantics of "icon" may be subjective, no quantitative research methods can be used to determine who is and is not iconic. Qualitatively, however, this text uses the word "icon" to refer to any individual who is generally seen to hold celebrity status, such as renowned worldly musicians,

Hollywood actors and actresses, elite professional sportspeople, highly influential online personalities among other titles of comparably likewise status.

Why do we have Icons?

The iconic purpose? Firstly, examples set by celebrity behemoths fortify desirable behaviour norms through popularising specific values. Second, the icons themselves trend-set both physical and emotional behaviours, meaning they cement the foundations for behavioural norms and how people should think. Third, craftily, Hollywood has often abused the popularity of icons to further national and political agendas, such as with John Wayne and his consistent personification of American power, to inspire Western audiences to conform to their new social norms.

Icons also have their immense wealth, influence, and skill glorified by their respective field source: Capitalist economies exalt their grandest earners. Social media companies will showcase the most popular user-creators, football organisations will reward their best players with individual honours. All these icons are used to demonstrate what one might achieve with perceived hard work in a respective industry, resulting in obsessive-compulsive manners in invested consumers who wish to obtain this social status for themselves. Inherently, as the consumers lust over their ambitious dreams, they consume more of the product being sold to them through iconic performances, perhaps being the dream itself.

Instinctively, humans will play follow the leader. The great leaders of humanity today are the societies in which humans live, the cultures they submit to, and worship the influences within these cultures. Icons have significant influence within Western culture and are displayed in every corner of society; people wish strongly to emulate these heroic figures as that is what they are supposed to do.

How do they maintain their fame?

Neo-Marxists might say that icons oppress those beneath them to remain dominant, starving the oppressed of precious opportunities to progress in their industry. Although Karl Marx did not personally account for status strata like Max Weber, Marx's theory of dialectical materialism does depict a conflict between two groups struggling for dominion, much like those who are famous and those who want to be (which is not everyone). Therefore, some credit should be levelled at this assumption as it is indeed plausible to suggest that a Hollywood actor has once before diminished the career prospects of an aspiring actress that they dislike via a conniving usage of their influence at the hallowed hierarchies in which they roam. However, this assumption is also short-sighted and generalising; for sure, not every icon has purposefully abused their distinguished powers to maintain their social position.

Asinine! Asinine is the belief that all icons wish only for their fame and all that comes with it. Take, for example, the misfortunate nature of child actors. How can it be claimed that these children wanted the heavy burdens whilst remaining too young to make an informed decision? How can it be claimed that many of these children wanted to subsequently spend their early adulthood devastated by psychotic disorders like schizophrenia or mood disorders like manic depression? Whilst these children did not maintain their careers, a degree of iconic status was immortalised by their tragic story, a story that they did not ask for. Thus, their iconic status may haunt them like individuals deemed internet memes; they become an icon at their own expense, a parody of sorts. Nonetheless, there shall be more writings on this later subject later in the chapter.

Reality television stars are often associated with a lack of intelligence. Sometimes, this is due to their own accord, other times due to their on-screen portrayal, and occasionally due to a pre-existing opinion on all reality TV icons. Intriguingly, these three factors interlope with one another, both consciously and unconsciously, affecting the actions of icons in telling them how they should act to maintain their status, irrespective of their identity. Problems arise here about identity, self-image, self-esteem issues with the icon (more on that later), and how the public perceives these icons regardless of their specific behaviours and personalities usually dictated by directors and screenwriters anyway. Hence, a retainment of fame here is achieved by an icon conforming to the desires of their senior staff who are once again selling a product. Naturally, the standard behaviours of a reality television star are what a show's audience has already bought into, so a performance adhering to that will lead to more significant consumer investment into the show and the icon. Unfortunately, individuals who adopt matching behavioural characteristics of reality television stars hoping to emulate their status will generally be associated with nothing but stupidity, and shunned. This is notably true when considering how ordinarily unattractive people treat attractive people possessing these driven personality traits, primarily out of envy, belittling their physically alluring counterparts. Although, the widespread opinion of the envious also depletes as a result, and they are ridiculed. To reiterate, the conflict created by the opposing character types is also a significant selling point of a reality television show as it tries to conjure heroic and villainous characteristics beneficial to the promotion of its product.

Some icons, like Olympic gold medallists, might be the best. However, whilst some countries have better development programmes than others, Western athletes are generally stratified by their physical ability to excel in their role. Therefore, athletes maintain their fame by outperforming their rivals in an equal environment.

By nature, icons thrive on the fandom demanded by their infectious personalities that provide endless openings for appearances in areas they do not belong to. In particular, television talk shows are permeated with icons distributing unqualified, harmful advice for the masses about crucial topics like intricate political movements, which should require professional guidance to comprehend fully. Instead, the bias misinterpretations spewed for the mouths of ignorant icons are encouraged and applauded, for the public are so infatuated by the iconic few that they unintentionally disregard the intellectual thinkers. They have spent decades mounting an excellent understanding of a theoretical discipline that will help them. So naturally, production companies prioritise harvesting economic wealth over the prospect of voicing solicitous support for all needing help in complex situations.

Deceitfully, icons may even steal the ideas of uninfluential people to sustain a consistent flow of influence devoid of repercussions. This discredits the great work of 'normal' people and deprives it of value. Conversely, it is not uncommon for people to ultimately credit important work to the iconic origin and claim that another 'normal' person's creation has been copied from an icon, once more indicating spiteful behaviour across the public upholding the gravity of icons.

Lavish Lifestyles

A vital element of the iconic way of life is the lavish lifestyle that comes with such tremendous status. Much like hummingbirds nesting atop tree branches, it is a commonplace to observe an icon in their habitual environment of glitz and glamour. However, the lavish lifestyles of the iconic few are presented to the general public in such a suggestive manner of superiority that it could be classified as callous. Whilst many icons are clearly drowning in their insatiable egos; perhaps some icons intend the mass showcasing of their immense wealth to be inspiring; however, their astute agents have no time for immaterial action and are bolstering the grand stature of their clients through public image manipulation and public relations, this is their job, after all, their expertise. Naturally, the depressing postulation of iconic gloating for the mere purpose of locking the peasantry out of hopeful mansions is certainly not mindboggling. Although, the hope remains...

Annoyingly, numerous celebrities appear contemptuous about fanatical obsessions with them, which is fine as a passive acceptance of paparazzi harassing them is terribly wrong. However, it becomes unfair when this contempt is of the fanatical people rather than fanaticism. Celebrities who are not born into fame should know better as they would have once fandom over those they currently imitate in the elitist sense. If they expect their fans to treat them as they would anyone else, they fail to consider the momentous way society portrays them compared to the little people who are taught to quake in their shadows.

Unobtainable Goals

Without lending excessive support to democratic socialism, the economic structure of capitalism, serving as the popular Western societal base today, causes excellent unrest in citizens of low social positions due to the seemingly impossible task they are unofficially burdened with of upward social mobility. Although the difficulty in doing so has lessened over time, people who hail from 'working class' (all socioeconomic class names are somewhat inaccurate) backgrounds achieving enough material wealth to upgrade the supposed quality of their life is a rocky journey. Understandably, the fact remains the same when speaking specifically of iconic status. Many icons already come from wealthy households, or if they do not, then they are usually traced to have been bestowed with great luck, especially when considering social media personalities who create content that aligns with an unappreciatively complex amplification algorithm or aspiring musicians who have bumped into established musicians and extraordinarily been gifted a helping mentoring and promotional hand. Categorically, insurmountable luck is perpetual to the attainment of fame. The idea that steadfast diligence will always be rewarded is an evil lie that characterises the current capitalist socioeconomic system, which links happiness to success, therefore telling the supposedly unsuccessful majority that they have no right to be happy when they must live with their perceived failures. Harmfully, many people's self-image weakens because of what they are told, and thus, their self-esteem is lower. Confidence moves with self-esteem, and if a person's confidence is too low for too long, they are likely to spiral into depression. As the legendary sociologist Emile Durkheim once noted, this heinous nature of capitalism carries the tendency to cause significant cases of suicide. Citizens of a capitalist society commit suicide because they are sold an unobtainable dream.

The icons are gifted with stardom that equipping them with immense cultural and material privileges. Hence, it is a shame to witness such iconic oddities disingenuously spout naïve rubbish like "be careful what you wish for" regarding the resource-deprived wishing for an easier life in a society entirely structured on capital. Astoundingly, the lowly majority must consider the path to their valued goals whilst simultaneously dealing with the demoralising petulant cries of the fortunate few. Dreamers will feel guilty when dreaming if they listen to those living the dream from which the Gods of the dream sold. Somewhat confusing, no?

Lack of Diversity

Concerning unobtainable goals, icons are repeatedly painted to have acquired a specific and highly beautified body image. Male icons are characteristically chiselled, muscular, and tall, while female icons adopt petite, fair, and smooth physical aspects. Correspondingly, society's shared norms hinge on the colossal popularity of these desired iconic features and champion their relative attractiveness. Unfortunately, persons not possessing these facets that brainwash others into senseless admiration are directly devalued and may become socially isolated. Therefore, they are forced to evolve their self-image by changing their identity to regain inevitably lost self-esteem and evade a likely spell of anxiety coupled with depression.

Expanding on the lack of socially diverse representation across the iconic realm, there is a scarce reason (aside from specifically particular persuasions) in choosing not to cast characters living with specific physical or mental disabilities such as Down's syndrome or autism spectrum disorder (ASD), although the former of which relies on a regressive and self-defeating illness diagnosis that will be covered in *Chapter Fourteen*. A person living with such a condition is more likely to disassociate themselves with the core message, despite its nobility, if they cannot relate to the characters personifying its values. Additionally, a greater volume of accurate representation is more likely to be captured by a performer who does live with conditions portrayed by their character, so the motives of production companies who employ iconic actors without normalised 'health' conditions for greater traction are contributing to the repellent social stigma surrounding people living with them which they amusingly claim to be challenging. Frustratingly, the vengeful backlash levelled by audiences is generally much tamer than that of the uproar colliding with a production company that "whitewashes" a film or television programme, perhaps because of the lesser people that feel they belong to the relevant social groups but definitely because of the shared norms and values in society greatly underrating the seriousness of disability representation to the mentality, recognition, and treatment of mental wellness completely across society.

At present, in Western stand-up comedy, a Christian, conservative, or culturally abnormal comedian is rarely successful on account of the blatant left-wing (excuse the cliché) political biases that counterintuitively plague the openly all-ridiculous entertainment genre due to oversensitivity, oversensitivity that contributes massively to the shaping of an unhappy society. Taking the previously mentioned Abrahamic religious group, for example, Christians are predictably overgeneralised as ludicrous, homophobic, right-wing extremists (laughably based on objectively differing interpretations of ancient text and acts of historical monarchies who twistingly abused Marx's "opium of the masses" for individual gain) for in for safe mockery by seemingly cloned comedians. As the societal resentment of Christians intensifies and encourages malicious behaviour, comedians are subconsciously manipulated into preaching their ironically irrational, irreligious ideals to their gullible audiences. Of course, these fallacious lectures of contempt negatively influence the audiences' perceptions of Christians in a strangely, unknowingly hostile, and unenlightening environment that has transformed from a place where ordinary people could escape their troubles and laugh to a line of idiot factories where icons feel compelled to unintelligibly endorse a social movement for five seconds of applause that their crowd is awkwardly prompted to provide. Therefore, the iconic comics of today distribute borderline discrimination (as it is clumsily yet officially defined) to particular social groups in the form of joke-like statements that carry a heavy agenda. However, these icons are puppets to their mechanical masters who unjustly dictate what people can and cannot say about what and who.

Power

Unmistakably, modern icons are worshipped in the Occident. Devout followers are deindividualised by their insatiable desires to be their icon instead of themselves and will ferociously defend their honour online or in-person with biting fury. Furthermore, some fanatics will refuse to consume even the slightest of an icon's product if their divinity has suffered a personal disagreement made public. Until recently, Chris Brown listeners would characteristically avoid listening to Drake's music due to the fallout between the goliath musicians. Fans of both icons would antisocially clash; the careers paths of the icons became both serviced and sabotaged in places. Regrettably, the individual welfare of fanatics is inconsiderately sacrificed by the icons and their agents to boost their economic and cultural power, setting a pathetic yet prominent example of attitude for the general public who are all exposed to the iconic powers in some sense. This perpetual socialisation origin a blinding obsession that occupies fanatics, so they remain oblivious to the highly unethical favouritism of icons in society.

Certainly, fanatics will copy character traits of their beloved heroes like behavioural attitudes, their sense of style, and their expressed beliefs. Thus, when an icon exhibits prejudice against a particular social group, their loyal admirers will likewise do so too. However, it should be explained that icons do not always intend to express their uninformed opinions surrounding sensitive topics, but they are so often used as commercial megaphones that are socially isolating, or polarising people has been nurtured into them.

Kanye West is a lyrical genius, but he would probably not make for a great president despite his talents. However, he still mustered a recognised campaign without any previous political experience. Of course, Donald Trump infamously rose from television personality to president, but he did so with a much more appropriate resume than the 'Louis Vuitton Don' with his vast experience in business which helped the US economically. However, Trump's presidency was overall not fruitful, especially when considering his negligent mishandling of the COVID-19 pandemic coupled with his failure to be re-elected versus Joe Biden in 2020. The point is that the presidential bid in Western democracies is simply a popularity contest rather than a talent contest (much to Socrates's projected disdain), and who is more popular than icons? The theory that celebrities are almost always incompetent in governing roles is supported through a brief analysis of their performances in such roles, but what is more important is the power they are provided with the tempts them to voice their embarrassingly unqualified political endorsements, dividing the masses and conjuring societal conflict for no reasonable cause. The insufferable self-importance of icons stemming from the receipt of fanatic veneration leads icons to categorically dismantle whomever they wish to by sending legions of fans to harass them online. Dangerously, celebrities granted such a volume of political power might amateur endanger entire societies with their misconceptions, incompetence, and inflated egos, driving them into causing inevitable disaster. Catastrophically, the ascension of celebrity power in politics indicates that absurdities such as rappers without college degrees passing legislation and commanding the armed forces are growing in likelihood and will only worsen.

As has been frequently mentioned, celebrities are God-like beings in a civilisation that revers futile obsessions rather than skill or virtue. For example, the surreal success of tabloid media proves the general public's infatuation with gossip surrounding the lucrative lives of other people that are entirely ignorant to their existences. Honestly, to become famous is to transcend the mundane reality of the commoner's realm.

Cancel Culture

'Cancel culture' is a phrase thrown around excessively by discredited conspiracy theorists and radicals looking to justify unjustifiable deeds, but it is also a movement destroying societal norms and values for the worse. Cancel culture aims to set dangerous moral precedents that suggest if an individual (usually demonstrated by an icon) makes a mistake, irrespective of when then they deserve to have their world destroyed so much so that they could never achieve nor strive for anything anymore as they are so objectively evil that they are unworthy of redemption. Hence, it is counterintuitive in its supposedly righteous intent as it sacrifices the importance of forgiveness to use one not-so precious life as an example of the repercussions of subjectively unacceptable actions, which results in a clouding of life's purpose for the cancelled people.

'Cancel Culture' is commonly disregarded as a nothing but a corny label used to denigrate justice, although, in reality, the phrase is very much representative of the mob's way of life (their culture), which is to destroy the life chances of their targets, essentially 'cancelling' them. Cancel culture is a mob culture, an inhuman Babylon of denizens that discourages independent critical thinking. The culture forces people to ascertain normalised beliefs out of fear of being cancelled, not virtuous intent; thus, the culture is paradoxically inspired by tyranny rather than social justice.

Unnaturally, cancel culture also requires participants to ignore any incidents where they may have said something discriminatory, despite previously recognising that these words do not define their social views when witch-hunting those that have. Therefore, cancel culture perpetuates hypocrisy.

<u>Iconic Wellbeing</u>

On the fifteenth of February 2020, British television presenter Caroline Fleck tragically committed suicide after receiving months of heinous abuse online. After the cancellation, the mob got wind of personal details in her previous relationship. Despite her ex-lover condemning the onslaught, the waves of death threats never ceased, and Fleck's self-image and esteem hit such a low that she felt that the only escape was actually to hang herself. The wicked brutality of cancel culture can foster serious mental health issues in icons, which some so easily forget are also human beings.

The awful trend of discontent in the iconic world is evidenced by the continuous fall of child actors. Whether it be the fact that these children suffer financial abuse perpetrated by their peers or that they receive hateful messages from disgruntled fans, child actors are historically insufficiently protected. Concerningly, the lack of supervisory responsibility taken for their welfare has infamously steered child actors to plummet into the abyss of irrelevancy once they outgrow their cherished youth. For example, Jake Lloyd, an American child actor, is diagnosed with paranoid schizophrenia and has spent residence inside a psychiatric facility after transference from jail. Lloyd's development of the psychotic disorder is heavily implied to be a cause of the bullying he received at the hands of classmates and fans, further fortifying the idea that fame, despite its clear benefits, does not always bring about happiness.

Consequent Mental Health Issues

Conclusively, suicide is a definite consequence of the way icons are treated in modern Western society. Icons are under constant spotlight and therefore pressured by insurmountable quantities of people who throw great expectations of behaviour at them; fanatics often develop depression after poor self-images for extended periods when forced to obsess over their quality of life that of the iconic few. Furthermore, a ruthless mob culture of mindless destruction creates a conflict through polarisation, thus spawning a dysfunctional society where redemption and self-improvement are meaningless. Weirdly, opposing parties (mobs vs icon reps.) prompt fanatics to both undermine iconic achievement yet obsess over it, destroying shared values which both parties rely on for their systems to function. Wondrously, this proves the absolute subjectivity of shared values. The less a man worries over the lives of others, the less he will worry at all.

Chapter Four: Entertainment

What is the Entertainment Industry?

The entertainment industry houses a distinct collection of iconic arts such as film, music, radio, publishing, and television (TV), all for the leisure of the public, whatever they may be interested in. Now wholly available from the comfort of one's own home, shows of comedy, horror, fantasy, and beyond have never been more popular thanks to the degenerated prominence of expensive cinema and theatre tickets. Although despite radio and TV sets pivoting a vitally accessible reception of broadcasted information, the internet now storms the entertainment industry with its unmatchable mass provision of content from all forms.

   The dominant aspects of the entertainment industry (and the focus of this chapter) are undoubtedly film and episodic serials. However, the sole attractions of prevalent on-demand video streaming services such as *Amazon Prime Video* and *Netflix* captured visions of Hollywood and the small screen instantly available in seemingly endless virtual libraries at the tap of a screen. Not only do these subscription-based giants represent the entertainment industry, but their usage has emerged so second nature that it is now a federal crime to 'steal' another person's Netflix account in the USA, so you better be careful the next time you borrow a friend's streaming privileges.

The nature of the content brought to ardent audiences across the West has changed significantly over the past century. As past eras dimmish, so too does the regularity in spiteful depictions of marginalised social groups shown in content; modern entertainment delivers more guts and glamour than ever before with a philosophical interest in social expression. Nevertheless, whatever the time may be, the entertainment industry has consistently produced 'safe' content that conforms to the normalised ideas of its social environment timeframe. So, naturally, people are entertained by what they are supposed to like.

How does it attract audiences?

Has one ever found themself feeling a profoundly personal connection to a fictional character that flawlessly immerses them into an imaginary world? By design, the Western entertainment industry looks to bring the deepest fantasies of the audience to life. From rags-to-riches heroes fighting off mythic beasts to romances of the most lustful origin, film and TV lives off the public's deepest desires. Consumers see themselves in these protagonists. That is why they need to succeed in their quests; if the good guy wins, so does the consumer.

Opportunistically, production companies will use current political movements to leech profit off of audience who already possess a connection with so the product is untasked with developing a technically good story that forges audience-character association. The product's narratives are often copied from previously successful stories, meaning that the newer unoriginal content mimics what is fashionable and further popularises their underlying messages.

The insipid mottos showbiz half-heartedly spouts at audiences often takes the form of pandering; thus, it is gleefully accepted as genuine social consideration. False political endorsements currently permeate the themes of Western film and TV shows using bogus techniques, such as forced diversity, to settle the wave of social unrest the reactionary 'liberal' showbiz consumers threaten to unleash should they witness the unforgivable crime of production companies daring to employ actors based on artistic talent or historical accuracy for the roles created to fit an elaborate narrative. Astoundingly, another method of evading cancellation is to maliciously mock other social groups. Of course, production companies will capitalise on easy targets like Christians and republicans as they are framed to directly oppose the pawned audience's collective values as well as the show's theme. However, social groups unloved by social justice factions fall victim to groups ceaseless mockery, unprotected. For example, *The X Factor* showcases its revered judges laughing at the expense of visibly disabled participants who admit they made an uninformed decision (these participants will usually infer that their "friends from work" told them they could sing) applying for an audition.

Furthermore, 'The Jeremy Kyle Show' collects people stewing in poverty whom they deem ripe for national ridicule. Whether it be their 'stupidity', physical appearance, promiscuity, or hygiene, the impoverished towns and cities where they hail are run by governing bodies responsible for the cultural and material resources available to them. So, blaming poor people for not engaging in more civilised or healthy lifestyles completely ignores the reality that their local areas are rifled with cheaper fast-food restaurants, air pollution, lower education standards, and a general lack of support beyond a fruitless welfare state. Their communities have been abandoned. How is that their fault? Why should audiences be encouraged to laugh at this degree of misfortune? Honestly, beyond 'old, straight, rich white men' equalling 'bad', hypocritical social justice warriors (forgive the cliché) are incapable of caring about oppressed social groups who have not been given the limelight because they lack the level of critical thinking needed to discover social inequalities for themselves and must be told what and whom to complain about as they are inherently conformist. Whilst middle-class perspectives cloud the opinions of liberal feminists, other antiliberals regress and already conflicted society via their refusal to consider a picture wider than that of pointless rebellion and vengeance. Similar to racist organisations like the Ku Klux Klan (KKK), the insatiably bigoted and harmful mentalities of extremists wishing to 'enslave all white people' or 'kill all men' (not that it is at all a genuine threat and despite their senses of humour appearance, these mindsets are more popular than you may know), which is mirrored in the radical mentalities of the resentful antiliberals who cannot get over earlier life as a rejected social outcast.

Excessive Misrepresentation

It is no secret that marginalised social groups will occasionally find themselves on the receiving end of misrepresentative content on film or TV that unfairly generalises the attitudes and behaviours of people belonging to that social group, whether it be for comedic effect or otherwise. Prevalent victims of excessive misrepresentation are Muslims, who are supplementarily vilified across the right-wing press. Brutally, these Islamic not only make up a minority in the Judeo-Christian societies but are characterised by a radical minority of Muslims who are usually located around Northern Africa and the Middle East, away from Islamic targets in the West. Depictions of social groups on film and TV influences the audience's general perception of these groups. Therefore, when Muslims are exclusively portrayed as nothing more than bloodthirsty fundamentalists who want to kill all the all-American heartthrobs, the content is endorsing sloppy misunderstandings of ancient scripture and contributing to the alienation of Muslims within the West. At present, it is next to impossible for Muslim immigrants to assimilate themselves into First World cultures when these nations are fed such fascist agendas; the stigmatising glorification of Islamic stereotypes only achieves to further the Western irreligious and xenophobic prejudices that utterly ignore how tyrannical Sharia countries have abused the sacred Quran as a control mechanism and that Muslims are (obviously) not inherently evil beings. Also, for those that say that they wish not for any religious characters to be included in the film and television shows (unless, of course, they are villainous zealots or corny comic relief) as "the products should be for everyone", the purposeful lack of religious 'representation' is exclusionary in itself. Nonetheless, the heinous level of misrepresentation would result in an uproar if applied to race, gender, or sexual orientation, so how is it fair to treat Muslims with such contempt?

Rather than LGBTQ+ minorities, another more minor talked about, but a perhaps more compelling case of misrepresentation spewed from the entertainment industry's ugly mouth is that of human sexuality itself. Biological experiments, social experiments, observations, and case studies consistently demonstrate that sexuality is fluid and can be classically and operantly conditioned as sexual orientation is essentially a socially learned societal construct. The oversimplistic overview of sexuality found in every corner of film and TV reinforces roles of sexual orientation that people subconsciously disagree over. Of course, nobody 'chooses' their sexual orientation as a cherry-picked lifestyle choice. However, it is simply impossible for anyone to be one-hundred per cent homosexual or one-hundred per cent heterosexual on the sexuality spectrum as that would implausibly concur with the existence of fixated psychosexual behaviour and cognitions. To expand, a person experiencing complete heterosexuality would have unconscious mental processes disabling an ability to recognise something 'attractive' in the same-sex, including themselves. Resultantly, they would burden an inconceivably low self-image regarding their physical appearance. Both the traditional and recently progressive views of sexuality seen in film and TV reinforce roles of sexual orientation that people subconsciously disagree over and cannot identify with; it alienates audiences and deprives them of valuably inclusive knowledge. Sexual orientation is just a private placement on an immeasurably broad spectrum, there are aspects of this that can and cannot be controlled, and the fluid nature of sexuality means that it can change, so do not ever feel guilty for "being greedy." Every individual is unique, and sexuality plays a great part in that, but it could never define one's own individuality.

Theoretically, accurate representation erodes any stigmatic prejudices directed at a social group. However, is it even possible to 'represent' an entire group of people?

The Fallacy of Representation

The most widespread understanding of social division representation in film and media inadvertently describes an ultimately positive portrayal that discourages the presentation of villainous characters played by actors from typically marginalised social groups, irrespective of any underlying messages. Moreover, this idea of representation seeks to stand for an empowering encapsulation of shared values in various communities. Thus it attempts to broadly assert the communal objectivity of subjective values claimed to be held by all members of a respective group. Although, the intrinsic subjectivity of the importance in portrayed values renders any attempt of collective representation obsolete as it forever remains impossible to accurately represent an entire group of people through one token character and their ungeneralisable ideals. Therefore, tying a group to subjective values unsympathetically deindividualises collective groups of people by ignores the differentiation in every single individual's ideological interpretations and valuations. Thus, this intentionally noble yet dysfunctional method of social representation can only be fallacious because of its counterintuitive discarding of paramount individuality. Here, representation conclusively requires a regressive method of generalisation that might leave a moderate portion of a collective embodied, but others indeed alienated from societal norms and ultimately socially isolated.

Despite one flawed understanding, the word 'representation' still holds steady gravity in the fight to empower members of marginalised communities. For instance, some say that if a social division has individual representations on all hierarchal levels, social equality can be claimed. So, if individuals in minority groups are shown that it is possible to reach the top no matter what, their feelings of empowerment and inspiration might boost their self-esteem and provide them with a hopeful foundation to build the life they want in a more equitable environment.

Universally Offensive?

Nothing is universally offensive. For instance, individuals hold individually subjective values to protect a person's way of life by making assumptions based on their appearance, which in itself could be offensive to that person. Thus, in order to be offended, a person must interpret that their personal beliefs have been attacked somehow, and any claims that what is said is objectively offensive to everyone deindividualises people as it ignores these contradicting values. To provide another example, an African-American might simply be offended by another person claiming that they ought to feel offended by a racial slur because they perceive this emotional fragility as a weakness: this is their opinion of an entirely subjective matter. Therefore, until society ceases to assert objectively offensive behaviours, the individual self-being will never be valued.

There is relentless pressure on producers to avoid offending anyone with their content material, which is, of course, an impossible task. Thanklessly, they pander to generalised assumptions of collective wants across minorities and unnaturally contort their product to leave any forced underlying messages feeling inauthentic. Uninspired methods of cultural accommodation such as this create an emotional disconnect between producers and consumers as it relegates empathetic thinking to a hypothetical type of insincere checklist-ticking; audiences will not relate to fictional characters on a personal level emotionally invested in a product that disregards natural emotional processes. However, this form of content is surging in popularity despite its ethical contradictions about generalisation and more. Why is this? Perhaps the audience feels a moral obligation to continue watching as they are tricked into believing that this content is tackling social issues like discrimination and inequality.

Citizens of the West are literally told to be offended by virtually anything, so oversensitivity must not be the public's fault. Globalism demands that people be courteous to foreign cultures but simultaneously fail to teach ways to equitably treat them as radical globalists perceive all foreign social groups to hold fundamental principles. Additionally, people who make up these groups are to be treated in the same way, hence cementing a philosophy set up to fail. Once people quickly realise the innate dysfunctions classifying societal conducts of behaviour, they become angry and confused as they cannot understand a correct method of intercultural diplomacy immediately after being diverted from the importance of humanism, which rightly disregards the characterisation of individuals via their apparent cultural positions.

Are you not entertained?

In Hollywood, virtual joy is brought to the audience by an employment process drenched in controversy. The #metoo movement, for all its false accusations and tokenism, has helped transition real social issues occurring even on the grand iconic scale. For example, an apparent pay gap between equally celebrated actors and actresses is accredited to gender, and scandals of repetitive sexual abuse have defined the miserable lives of actresses inside patriarchal Hollywood. Disgraced American film producer Harvey Weinstein was convicted of multiples sex offences in 2020 that was driven into the limelight by the heroic forces of the #MeToo social media campaign, whereby over eight brave women in Hollywood were accused Weinstein of sexual misconduct. Meanwhile, this valiant display of social justice spawned the "Weinstein Effect", where newly empowered survivors of rape from all corners of the world would speak up about the horrifying torment that they were subjected to. Incredibly, these victims would now serve as an inspiration for those who had suppressed their trauma out of fear of being overshadowed by the dominance of man, as they truly lived in a man's world. Today, the conflict emerging exploding from within Hollywood may have boosted the mental wellbeing of some sexual abuse survivors now that they know they have a voice that will be heard, but what does the future hold? Considering society's obsessions with deindividualising collectivism and degrading victimhood, who knows? Although one thing is for sure, nobody should ever be scared of opening up as if they do choose to cry out, people are now receptive enough to hear their pleas.

Chapter Five: Mass Media

A Brief History

Mass media has remained an integral piece to the jigsaw of Western culture for loyal services to many of our collective society's traditional values of democracy, intellectual growth, and individuality. From fifteenth-century European popular prints, information on past and current events have graced consumers through mass communication, influencing their behaviours and attitudes by altering political perceptions and social stances. Information is indeed a powerful tool.

Mass media has played a catalyst role in the most important events in Western history. Capitalising on the power of public appeal, organisations have claimed power through inspiring societal developments of many kinds through all types of social movements: alternative, redemptive, reformative, and revolutionary. For example, in 1963, the frontman of the civil rights movement Martin Luther King Jr. provided a dynamic spectacle is perhaps the most infamous public speech of all time, where he would preach his dream of racial equality to an erupting crowd of over 250,000 supporters on the steps of the symbolic Lincoln Memorial, and an audience of millions more watching at home. Hence, the admirable activist's efforts for legislative change in the 1964 Civil Rights

Act's passing outlawing public discrimination of many social groups.

As mentioned in chapter two, the world got its first public radio broadcast in 1910, thanks to American inventor Lee de Forest. This revolutionary technological advancement eventually allowed mass marketing campaigns, major news stories and propaganda to be quickly and consistently distributed, devoid of the hassle of physical production and manufacturing costs for media companies and the purchase and collection of material goods for consumers. Meanwhile, following the events of WW2, television became domestically popular in the West, enabling further electrical advertisement, entertainment, and enlightenment.

What is the purpose of mass media?

So, we have established that mass media is used to communicate information to the masses for a variety of virtuous purposes, but what if any other goals? Are the functions of mass media exclusively honourable? Conversely, they seem to be far from it. Throughout the entirety of its existence in Western culture, mass media has thoroughly remained a business prospect. As evidenced by today's tabloid, each media outlet has an agenda to appeal to a select target audience. To expand, British daily newspaper *The Daily Mail* offers a clear conservative or right-wing bias, whereas *The Guardian* blatantly provides the inverse, labour or left-wing bias. These biases are utilised by the news outlets to capture and retain consumers who share that same bias. As with the willingness to sacrifice impartiality for a more loyal ('loyal' meaning more likely to be a returning customer) set of consumers, outlets often struggle to come by authentic news often enough to match their competition in the market consistently. Therefore they resort to less authentic means of media production, but we will get to that.

Another historical purpose of mass media is propaganda. Effectively used to incite international prejudice and hatred during wartimes, its Machiavellian means have less than deferred in recent times. Of course, within Western culture, outright discrimination on a front cover would stick out like a sore thumb, so what if it were not so vivid? However, the underlying messages of far too many articles are inherently troublesome. Casting our minds back to May 2018, concerning English football player Raheem Sterling and the curious case of his gun tattoo, nationally treasured(!) tabloid newspaper *The Sun* is rather uncharacteristically criticised for alleged racist motivations when publishing an article ridiculing Sterling for his tattoo. Critics noted the tabloid's association of Sterling gun tattoo and his ethnicity with the increasing use of firearms by British street-gangs recent to the time of publication, of which many are black. Now, whether *The Sun* were derogatively linking an endorsement of gun violence to the professional footballer due to the colour of his skin is irrelevant as the article's alleged insensitivity towards stereotyping made many people feel stigmatised and uncomfortable and understandably so. The UK government has adopted a progressive stance on limiting certain areas of communication to prevent discrimination (see the Equality Act 2010); this includes stereotyping members of protected social groups. This could explain why British people are typically so quick to identify discrimination as the government has theoretically led by example for citizens to emulate. Nevertheless, a rise in intolerance of social inequality has birthed the emergence of cancel culture, as previously discussed in *Chapter Three*.

Fortifying the deceptive nature of Western mass media is the existence of tabloid newspapers and magazines themselves. Similar to the bourgeoise's deceptive usage of football as the working man's sport intending to distract the proletariats of the economic oppression surrounding them, it could be assumed that the celebrity gossip that permeates tabloid media serves a greater purpose: to distract us from the psychological horrors of our daily lives.

Socialisation

Mass media has proven to be an effective method of gaining social unity and cooperation to strive for a shared value. Take the civil rights movement as a prime example, but what other powers does it hold? Given the growing popularity of lip-fillers in correlation with advertised glamour models donning the same look, mass media should be credited as the cause of this aesthetic trend and subsequently newly constructed social norms and values related to fashion desirability of bigger lips for females. As the cliché goes, correlation is not causation. However, they are not mutually exclusive terms and do not conflict in this case. Furthermore, as mass media holds power to change factors of social order (a topic for an upcoming chapter), it is thus able to change the fabric of society itself.

Fake News

Now that we have established that mass media is an extraordinarily influential tool, let us analyse how governments can abuse it to manipulate society into conformity with its ideologies.

'Fake news' is a term that virtually everybody in modern Western culture is sick of. Regrettably, it is also one of this chapter's reading topics. Think of fake news as a disease infecting its readers that spread the infection to others through retweets, reposts, and shares. Craftily, fake news feels very appealing to its target audience because the said audience is readily retained through constant agendas not-so secretively sold by the media machine. Naturally, if one is going to lie, they should make it a white one; fake news is generally quite audacious, rarely failing to capture the attention of both those overjoyed and disgusted by its contents. According to the modern-day algorithm, every click pays, so media outlets will attempt to accumulate as much of these as possible.

As inferred to previously, it is not uncommon for a news outlet to resort to fake news when exhausted of authentic news in order to retain audiences, rival competition, keep the cash flow coming, and supplement pre-existing agendas. However, this raises drastic ethical questions as news is unsurprisingly interpreted as factual by its readers, so any individuals vilified within fictitious articles could be slandered by mobs of devout consumers and have their livelihood ruined. There have been many examples of such shameful occurrences, one such case being of *Fox News*. This right-wing news outlet has since stated that they regret altering existing images to infer the threat of gun violence and using an image of a burning city that they wrongfully attributed to Black Lives Matter protests in Seattle, which they condemned for violence despite the protests being peaceful. With their sensationalist media coverage conjuring a climate of fear, Fox News was heavily criticised for contributing to the appearance of armed unrest.

Extremism

Extremism is a term that generally refers to a radical or 'far' leniency to an ideological concept, take political extremism, for instance, a far-right media outlet like Breitbart News in the US publishes new stories that champion traditionally capitalist values and simultaneously belittle the inverse of communism, or at least its more popular sister, socialism. This means that whilst it ironically carries an extremely intimidating degree of heaviness with its mere morphology, extremism is widespread in Western mass media. It is a tool used by publishers to further polarise the masses, often by transferring their extreme intolerance of the reverse political spectrum onto the contents of their product, poisoning the minds of its readers to conform with a particular set of ideological values and reinforce their existing corresponding beliefs, whether there be anti-socialist or anti-capitalist, political differences and conflict are frequent outcomes of extremism in the media. Why, in any case? Well, as mass media outlets have their agendas, they also have their own loyalties. Politicians are habitually observed to favour media outlets that agree with them; thus, they form a relationship. This is dubbed the 'politico-media complex', which had rising prevalence in the very early twenty-first century in European countries that gradually fell through the Reporters Without Borders' annual 'press freedom index' rankings for the restrictions levied on the press in its right to criticise the government. Although, this is more common in the rest of the world.

Resilience and a willingness to disengage is discouraged both individually and collectively by extremist media outlets. The strengthening of the reader's pre-existing biases causes the reader to develop more extremist points of view in line with the media's ideological, political, or social beliefs and tend to act out public support for these principles. This process is called radicalisation.

<u>Radicalisation</u>

Contrasting with extremism, radicalisation is how a person's principles shift to support drastic societal change, not the actual extremist values. Whilst, radicalisation does not necessarily mean that physical or emotional violence is inevitable, a radical person's criminal orientation more increase as the ideological goals they wish to achieve become more essential to their lives and anti-social behaviours towards members of stigmatised social groups come hand in hand with a belief in what extremist media generalises to consumers about the opposing principles and the people that hold them. For example, a far-right mass media outlet reporting on the rising level of knife crime in London may refer to the criminal perpetrators as "youthful" and "urban", leading many traditionalist conservative readers to associate this with stereotypes of members of social groups who may have been generalised to be violent previously by the media outlet, per its agenda. This hypothetical scenario (although it sounds all too familiar) would stimulate any readers' above-average potential for racial intolerance and generate racism. Resultantly, the readers would collectively socially isolate an entire social group, seeking to marginalise individuals with black skin through social stigma. Patently, people can be stigmatised in many ways: the way they look can be ridiculed, cultural differences could be alienated.

Meanwhile, discrimination of this social group becomes so commonplace that it is normalised into society's social order, and even the social disorder as rates of hate crime will undoubtedly skyrocket. Social norms and values become finer. Therefore society regresses and becomes less socially diverse.

In contribution to the consequent degeneration of social inclusion within society, the opportunistic mass media will continue to manipulate the masses with extremist propaganda, overwhelming more progressive competitors who have their messages of empowerment silenced by hordes of discrimination. Additionally, this product will sell well as it garners more and more of an audience with the rising popularity of discriminatory attitudes and behaviour. How will the media stay on top and continue to sell when every other popular media outlet is equally extremist? The answer, they will be more extreme! Clickbait, gossip, fake news; anything for the sterling, euro, or dollar. Tragically, as more negative deceptions of targeted social groups appear in media, the higher the hostility towards them, which is a cycle that will not stop with a mass uprising to combat the oppression, like the civil rights movement, which is primarily possible through mass media, the one who rules them all.

Consequent mental health issues

Imagine Chelsea. She has a physical disability. Irrespective of where she finds herself, she has a target on her back. A target that is hit with multiple shots of discrimination daily, attacking many different components of what makes Chelsea a part of her community. At target, that must read 'different', 'ugly', 'lazy', 'unwanted', or 'kick me emotionally'. She notices that she is not treated as an individual; there are no person-centred considerations towards her. Sure, Chelsea may hear the odd message of support deriving from the comfort of an ivory marketing tower, but this is probably just tokenism used to stand a brand out. Nobody cares about her because Chelsea is Chelsea. People only see her disability and think what the media tells them to think or what others groups say about disabled people online for amusement. 'Why is this happening to me?' you ask yourself. So, Chelsea looks at herself, and she looks at them, and she is showered with guilt. Any deviation from the norms of this 'enabled' society becomes an imperfection, a problem, a defect. She notices the physical inapparencies right away, but is that all? Her use of language, her interests, her status... are these problems too? Chelsea wonders: "How do I change, how do I conform to societies shared values and norms, how do I fit it?" This society fails to realise that everybody is individual, therefore different, but Chelsea does not see that as she cannot. Suddenly, it hits Chelsea, a solution to her wellbeing, an escape from the oppressive grips of this nightmare. She cuts herself away from the outside world; nobody can target her where they cannot see her.

Meanwhile, as she sits alone, just Chelsea and her thoughts, she realises just how little she is accomplishing; she is throwing her life away. Sure, the alternative of venturing outside of her now exceedingly fragile comfort zone will be met with disdain from others, but at least a chance at life presents itself. Or does it? What options will Chelsea have if she ventures back into the big wide world? Her options are minimal; others seem to be unified in what she perceives as their hatred towards her and her defining characteristic.

Chelsea thinks to herself, "even with legislation protecting my disability, I am not protected." As she ponders this, her phone lights up. A new media article, permeating with the same generalising content about stay at home (which is now all the more upsetting), benefit frauds she thought she had escaped, but there is no escape as these are the significant factors of the society in which Chelsea lives. Time passes, and she is doing worse than ever; Chelsea may have no friends or family that she feels she can reach out to; Chelsea only has herself along with her increasingly poor self-image. She feels the last remnants of her self-esteem begin to slip away, for Chelsea has only exposed herself to negative portrayals of her perceived self, and now these horrific messages have deluded her mind into believing in truth to fallacy. Low self-esteem is a natural path to depression, which commonly occurs with anxiety. Chelsea has become too anxious to seek help and is too depressed to see a way back. She must seek a method of recovery, but how?

According to many recent studies, disabled people are four times more likely (on average) to commit suicide than their nondisabled peers. If we truly lived in a socially diverse society, then this would not be the case. As the forefront of the spread of information to the masses of society, mass media can change this horrifying statistic by empowering disabled people for their traits, ignoring the social group. Our mindsets are dictated by the media we consume. If they are virtuous, then so are we.

Chapter Six: Social Media

What is Social Media?

The phrase 'social media' refers to interactive online services that provide a social platform for communication through digital media expressions. Contrary to mass media, social media centralises the formally passive audience and personalises the content that appears on their 'feed' according to their expressed interests. Additionally, social media platforms enable users to instantly interact with each other at will with the innovative invention of comment sections, coupled with advanced implementations of direct messaging. Conclusively, apps and websites with these functions also develop a surging potential for brand exposure that allows businesses to develop using attention generated by conversation.

Like it or not, social media's popularity means that it is a stable method of communication, entertainment, and marketing in the twenty-first century. By allowing users to exchange various information worldwide, social media outlets provide digital community bases that have generated a sizable array of beneficial opportunities. These superlative social 'shortcuts' include conveniently reviving diminishing friendships, reconnecting with extended lost relatives, discovering highly recommended products and services, advertising otherwise hidden products and services, charitable intercommunal contributions, or even exchanging life-saving advice and support. Magnificently, such essentialities are all made possible due to the hybrid 'social plus media platform' that the online outlet offers.

Social media is a dualistic utopia and dystopia; its fluid ability to rapidly influence the topics of communal conversations can both enhance or derail the shared perception of a popularised topic. By design, social media algorithms encourage communication, but communication can quickly turn very sour. Destructively, the social part of social media results in mass conformity as attention-seeking users will very often voice controversial statements to bait reactionary users, who themselves will be showered with support for their abusive comments made against the original poster. Concurrently, attention-seeking behaviour is secretly endorsed by social media companies because posts garnering more reactions are boosted by algorithmic sequences to their impression counts. Therefore users copy these post-popularity methods to receive the attention they so desperately crave at the cost of being cyberbullied. However, the gifts brought forth by social media outlets are not without their shortfalls, speaking of which...

Interpersonal Communication

As mentioned in *Chapter Two*, the populous' general interpersonal communication skills have plummeted since the popularisation of social media, presumably resultant of the ensnaring nature of social media and its convenient ability to provide a base for social connection online, which is now the primary method of communication for the bewitched Generation Z (zoomer) populous.

Thriving upon the culture wave of manipulation, social media algorithms cast their maniacal magic to fixate a user's laser attention onto their phone screen so much so that it cannot be diverted. Unscrupulously, trickster advertisements and clickbait articles will sneak themselves into the zombified subject's newsfeed whilst they remain in their vulnerably docile state. At the same time, the zombie continuously succumbs to interaction prompts on posts that are exclusively selected to be shown on their personalised newsfeeds, based on both their expressed and silent media preferences. Some of these interactions prompted on conversation stirring posts involve 'commenting' or 'tagging', whereas other posts with simplistic yet potent messages need only to be 'shared' to grouped acquaintances, all of which, to zoomer jubilation, remove the trouble of taking the time and effort to physically meetup and speak to others. After all, why would anybody neglect such fantastical inventions which slaughter the oppressive barriers of space and time to communication?

Furthermore, those who dwell in the bowels of agonising anticipation need not languish in awaiting responses anymore, for these social platforms also do the kind courtesy of alerting users as to when their friends are typing out responsive comments, then again instantaneously playing the profane subaudition that user-attention must be glued to continue their communications and status, as without likes and replies a user cannot esteem any online status. Hence, parties will also have full-blown conversations in comment sections rather than together, as is 'natural'. Besides, supplementary system notifications lure zombies back the narrowminded embracement of digital talk, but at the severe cost of enforcing bizarre thought patterns onto them, which may not cost as much as the cryptic media machine. To illustrate, a person waking up at 06:00 may immediately check their phone and see notifications from a friend who stayed up late last night liking media posts whilst they were asleep, meaning that not only will the person waking up now be drawn into a digital trance of mass information rather than prioritising essential activities like getting washed, dressed, and fed, but their newly-nocturnal friend focused on depriving themselves of sleep in order to consume more overstimulating media. Thus, aside from the blatant ethical concerns raised here, the dominions of sufferance that are social media platforms unpractically fossilise and irregulate the need for interpersonal communication in a society that borders on postmodern with an apocalyptic disregard for social physicality. Consequently, the conformist zoomer populous essentially loses their collective interpersonal communication skills for lack of practice. When placed in a situation where they are needed, they become socially inept as their zombification has dominated their lives and stimulated their social anxieties.

Psychological Effects

It is plausible to suggest that because social media is structured in such a significantly manipulative way, zoomers have had their behaviour classically conditioned through extreme consumption. Specifically, interaction notifications function as the stimuli in which users unconsciously associate with the reward of a dopamine hit. Therefore, social media is essentially a drug that chemically induces the mind and behaviour of human beings by catalysing dopamine deficiency and ADHD, causing addictions and subsequent withdrawal symptoms, and artificially optimising vital psychological connections.

Man built the social media machine to be independent and self-organised via the adaption of AI, a technology that has now evolved further than man, who can no longer control it. Why though? Perhaps this is because AI relies on quantitative analysis on data, particularly probability, which it uses to determine what posts users are most likely to interact with based on data collection. If a user is shown posts that interest them continuously, they will find it challenging to resist returning to their newsfeed. Ethically, this method of addiction is incapable of accounting for the inhumane lack of morality involved in causing addictions; the AI only 'cares' about what will make the product more financially efficient and successful. Expanding on the troubling psychological aspects of AI usage, a user's posts will often be shown to people with matching data to boost interactions. However, when an audience rises into the hundreds and thousands, the original poster should become accustomed to being the recipient of hundreds and thousands of opinions levelled at their post they hold so dear, which humans are not evolved to deal with. Naturally, the constant dosage of social approval taking the forms of comments, likes, and shares mutates into something that zoomers cannot live without. Therefore they stay on social media, attempting to regain this social approval for evasion of feeling invalid.

The more a user lives and procrastinates on social media apps, the more they are overstimulated by rapidly interchanging types of content that fatigue them. Subsequently, the unproductivity resultant of their ironically antisocial dwelling typically brings about demotivation and shame in the users, as they guiltily realise that they are glued to their screens. Such discontent causes low self-esteem, and if not dealt with, can merge into mood or anxiety disorder like depression. In reprimand for causing these disasters in wellness, company heads like Jack Dorsey of Twitter have even been forced to apologise for the unhealthy designs of their social media products. Nevertheless, what progressive changes have these timid actions forged?

Validation Optimisation

Online media platforms house a plethora of personal highlights. To illustrate, posters usually choose to selectively post information that showcases their achievements, but not the more insipid happenings of their daily lives. Unsurprisingly, these boastful displays are often interpreted by audiences as the original poster's literal lifestyle, collectively stirring up unrealistic expectations by audiences in regards to the average quality of life, together with a defensive dissociation from reality as a coping mechanism to deal with irrational comparisons made by audiences in regards to themselves and the original poster, to evade feelings of social invalidity amongst their peers.

Continuing the lambaste of digital mass communication, the ostensible validation optimisation the 'like button' generates can only be rationally regarded as harmful to the emotional welfare of social media users. 'Likes' equate to value. Furthermore, those amassing the most likes are esteemed by those without to have obtained some degree of greatness, perhaps even bordering on perfection, as millions of likes perceivably signal millions of people gawking in admiration. More prominently, however, the volume of wide social approval levelled at a poster increases the more their post is liked; social approval is unfortunately highly regarded in Western society. Such toweringly high levels of peer admiration habituating the average newsfeed often illude users to the sheer unattainability of virality and teach them to care about what everyone thinks to the extent of peer approval being a fundamental necessity to maintaining a healthy self-image. In line with the rise in social media usage over the past decade, cases of depression and anxiety have skyrocketed in a manner that only a mindless fool could credit to coincidence. Tragically it could even be claimed that these services are killing people as a similar pattern is generally seen with teen suicide, conceivably because young people are sold normalised images of 'objective' beauty based on shared values, which are of course individually subjective. For instance, the term 'Snapchat dysmorphia' is coined to describe kids wanting to look like animated beauty filters that contort their faces unnaturally to hide imperfections and reshape their jawlines, amongst other things. These filtered images are popular because they glorify the typically desirable physical traits commonly seen in icons, giving the filter user more robust emotional security in the quality of their image, but also alienating them from their face as the image does not depict their face anymore more than it does a filter. Therefore it is the 'filter' that receives likes rather than the person.

Unbeknownst to the average user who considers iconic beauty to be a realistic goal, many online influencers utilise beautification filters to simulate a more alluring appearance, meaning users will continue to dwell on their low numbers of optimised self-worth when uploading unfiltered selfies despite their lack of audience interactions being consequential of a mixture of their much smaller audience and less contortionist behaviour. Additionally, this like count kindly serves as a public display of popularity that makes comparisons between peers easy. For example, a popular schoolchild posting a filtered selfie will almost always receive more likes than a less-popular classmate posting an unfiltered selfie. These validation statistics have staggering effects on the posters' mindsets and ultimately reinforce the polarising dominant and submissive social roles commonly seen in schools.

One of the social media's grandest attractions is the potential it provides for anyone to become a star, and numbers can measure stardom: followers, likes, comments, shares, and more. Unscrupulously, users look to grow these quantities as they desperately toil for the dangling prize of internet fame, adopting less honest tactics along the way. Acknowledging that inspirational acts of kindness are suitably met with enormous adoration and can grow fanbases, online creators are notorious for 'click-baiting', copying, or even staging videos of themselves performing charitable acts like giving away money to homeless people, but deviously using paid actors in their place. These fake personalities are smeared overzealously across social media to such an extent that any uplifting underlying messages are relegated into nothing more than insipid clichés, classifying the behaviour conveniently filmed for online purposes as thoroughly individualistic and increasingly so over time.

Surveillance Capitalism

Social media platforms commodify their unwitting users' personal data and sell it to advertising companies for profit; this emerging scheme for profit is coined as 'surveillance capitalism' by both academics and former social media employees that understandably leftover ethical concerns. Platforms massively collect data that advertising companies use to predict who will be the most inclined to purchase enticement, meaning that surveillance capitalism functions not really to sell on data, but people instead, as prospective customers. To illustrate, a user's interests, personal history, and location (all examples of valuable data) are sold to companies that are searching for potential buyers with compatible characteristics with their ideal buyers, say users who like many posts and pages centred on football will be shown adverts for football merchandise. Designedly, data handling is carried out devoid of human supervision, and whilst even a devout reader might have grown tired of hearing "the sinister horrors of AI" by now (my apologies if so), so the potential discomfort relentless, pushy ads heap onto users is entirely disregarded due to AI's incapacity for empathy. Manipulatively, people living with delicate insecurities might be recommended beauty products to 'fix' them, which certainly poses the careless risk of plummeting their self-assurance. Again, data is used to build predictions about the likelihood of user actions and devise dopamine targets related to these predictions to simplify finding potential buyers and drive up the customer's urge to return for more products, usually by inhumanely preying off of their insecurities. Overall, the objectifying process of surveillance capitalism can only be regarded as a threat to the mental health of the Western populous, because of course, attention can be mined, but humanity is not unrenewable.

Antisocial Media

By its dependence on like counts, outward appearances, and reactionary mobs, social media perpetuates judgement of others, furthered by its encouragement of conformity, deindividualisation, and personal comparisons. As discussed in *Chapter Two*, this judgemental culture coupled with a regulatory lack of user identification systems predictably makes opportunistic grounds for anonymity and cyberbullying, which is especially effective at striking fear into victims' hearts via the resident mob mentality culture afflicting social media. To the misery of many social media users, anonymity gifts such venomous imbeciles with the ability to pleasure themselves with a risen 'no holds barred' level of dark humour, usually a savage form of targeted mockery, without repercussions. This 'gloves off' sense of humour creates problems when jokers become abusers that target potentially sensitive information about a person, such as having a recently deceased relative or belonging to a particular social group, which they can feed off should they be incited. Unfortunately, provocation seems a susceptible process online that occurs in people by even the slightest of opposition, although this is not necessarily the fault of any quarrelsome individuals. Twitter, for example, wants users to make controversial and outlandish statements. Otherwise, it would not limit users to a measly 280 characters per 'tweet' (a small number only recently doubled from 140). Twitter knows that people who spend considerable time scrolling around on digital newsfeeds probably have short attention spans due to gradual overstimulation. Therefore it encourages short and impactful content production that appeals to people, who are also likely to redistribute this information and produce more of their own. However, any informative post requiring elaboration is restricted and reduced to something that has to capture a scroller's attention quickly (to guide them down a well-thought-out thread of linked ideas), a task that people tend to complete by voicing fiery and often insulting claims and oversimplistic ultimatums that barrage ideologists, rather than ideologies. Users see these petulant absolutes, and their responses are immediately split into two categories: the 'for' and 'against', who are both far more unpleasant than they may sound. Staggeringly, the 'against' brigade resort to abusing the original poster, commonly taking inspiration from some of the previously listed tactics of cyberbullies, whereas the 'for' team offer a variety of feedback that typically includes intentional misinterpretation and subsequent overuse of any underlying messages, scarce as they might be, or supplementary abuse of the opposition. Whilst Twitter (or anywhere else on the internet) may not boost the housing of any debates of the century, its contribution to online polarisation and antisocial behaviour is so potent that it has to be described as disgusting. Social media functions to decentralise individuality and champion mob-mentalities; it functions despite the diversity and emits a contagious allergy to independent critical thinking.

Not only can people's real-world behaviour be affected by it, but the conflict injected into people online is a recipe for radicalisation. Social media hinges on postmodernism, where there is no objective truth, and people can forever go back and forth, living with their facts and subsequently dwelling on their endless feeds riddled with personalised 'fake news' propaganda that sustains their divisive delusions. Different, unsubstantiated conspiracy theories dominate timelines depending on a respective user's recorded biases, where the algorithm sends them down a rabbit hole of related identity politics, reinforcing their pre-existing biases. Whether social media authorities use politics to keep users locked onto their services, stimulate agendas for affiliate politicians, or maybe they have just lost control of their product, maniacal extremist nonsense continues to plague timelines, recruiting regiments of radicals devoted to intellectual perversities like the notorious *#Pizzagate*, striving only to stir hatred for their socially dialectical enemy.

As determined by its inhumane algorithm, social media bares in intrinsic bias towards controversial, false information as controversy and conversation come hand in hand, and of course, more conversation means more usage, which means more capital profit for all. However, the polarising controversy as seen on social media spawns tribal warfare, a global attack on democracy that destabilises the orderly social fabrics of societies. For proof, look no further than the hate campaigns powered by social media in 2016 regarding the Russia-Trump coalition that led to interference in a presidential election, undermining the 'people's vote'.

Due to a flawed reliance on quantitative data analysis, mere modifications to the regulatory AI will not cure social media of its antisocial ills. AI cannot censor fake news; therefore, to avoid further societal damage, cultural and ideological shifts are essential. Specifically, there is a need to abolish the postmodernist fallacy of ultimate subjectivity; objective truth is not a manifestation of individuality or a social construct. Some things are simply factual. If society cannot define the fundamental needs of society, then the West will continue to ignore the challenges of climate change, discriminatory behaviour, mental health, and practically any other serious problem that collectively affects the human race.

Chapter Seven: Materialism

A Dystopian Utopia

Materialism, or economic materialism, is more of a personal attitude than a philosophy. Also, it is not to be confused with naturalism, a philosophy based on the immeasurable assumptions that there is nothing beyond the natural world and that no supernatural forces have influenced nature. Rather, materialism can refer to either a personality trait or a personal value. For example, a materialistic person's life ambition may be to acquire as many valuable physical possessions as possible, or they may be envious of people with more wealth in material goods than them. Crucially, materialism is concerned with the importance of economic resources rather than anything of an immaterial essence, such as love. Consequently, it is a vague topic area that can be studied in several forms.

Materialism is commonly connected to capitalism due to the similar ideals of materialists and capitalists. For example, capitalists believe that capital should form the basis of the socioeconomic system. With a 'free market' and other economic liberties, anyone can earn enough capital to live a lavish life, provided they are materialistic enough to be motivated by the collation of capital. Additionally, materialism is closely related to consumerism, which encourages people to become and perceives themselves to be consumers and customers of goods and services. Due to inflation and a culture of consumption in the West, the cost of these goods and services are continually increasing. Hence, consumerism is viciously criticised for its ability to manipulate people into debts, promote substandard conditions of labour, and industrial contribution to pollution via the 'need' for mass production of goods. This is what separates 'The American Dream' from the American reality.

Materialistic people are especially vulnerable to consumerism and are essentially why it makes so much profit for corporations, notably those who have cemented a 'luxury' brand name. For example, people who wear clothes from luxury fashion designers are materialistic. Whatever their reason may be, brand name, the high quality of linen, or to increase their self-perception, a person choosing to wear luxury fashion always has an inflated sense of worth for what is marketed as a luxury product and is therefore prepared to pay more money for them. Hence, the idea that some material goods can increase one's social status is why people infatuation with these goods. Although, it is important not to judge people with such crudely materialistic mindsets, for they are made that way due to their consumerist environment.

In a society with a capitalist ecosystem, people are measured by their economic assets. For example, they are sometimes placed in social classes according to their material wealth and are provided with different life opportunities according to these socially constructed classes. Therefore, in order to function within society, one must be materialistic. Should they not, then a lack of carefulness with their money, or a willingness to work for it, could lead to bankruptcy or poverty. Resultantly, the personal freedoms capitalism 'gifts' to society mean that people are perceived to have sole responsibility for their economic status because anyone can make it in a free market (undoubtedly). So, should a person be poor, they should make to feel ashamed as their failures have led to their suffering, and the sheer potency of this shame will overwhelm any spiritual security they might find in the immaterial. Losers can indeed have nothing else to blame in the capitalist utopia.

Greed

Greed is the emotional desire to obtain masses of wealth, regardless of the needs and wellbeing of others. It is related to materialistic feelings of selfishness and self-importance and will usually lead to cruelty. Despite the existence of greed before the industrial revolution, as evidenced by its listing as one of the 'seven deadly sins', Marx argues that class conflict, caused by dialectical materialism, has intensified feelings of greed in modern society. Whilst dialectical materialism has been a prominent component of his conflict theory since societies of hunters and gatherers, Marx claims that the ruling classes' unique methods of oppressing the proletariat have caused greed in every corner of the West. The bourgeoisie, the ruling class, mostly comprised of aristocrats and business owners, feel that they must maintain their economic dominance of the working-class, the proletariat, to preserve their high quality of life. Therefore, they trap the proletariat into working for small hourly wages, guaranteeing that they cannot afford an education that will give them opportunities for better occupations, and they alienate workers from their work which they know is worth more than them, ensuring that they are too demoralised and demotivated to strive for social mobility. Ultimately, the ruling class will safeguard their lives, in the name of greed birthed from materialism, via some of the vilest psychological means possible.

First World Problems

Every blessed Westerner will have been a reminder of their opulent privilege that they do not live in a Third World country whereby society is so underdeveloped that inhabitants will kill each other for a cup of water, or something like that. Europeans, North Americans, and some Oceanic few are told that they are lucky to live in a world that can meet their physiological needs, but who is saying this? Well, surprise, surprise, it must be those blasted materialists again. Not having to worry about starving or getting killed by a lion on a twenty-mile trip for a bucket of water is a privilege, obviously. However, the Western world creates problems for its citizenry. For example, happiness correlates with success until a certain point, and suicide rates are far more common for people stewing around in poverty (see *Chapter Eleven*). Granted, correlation is not causing, but, with logic, one should conclude that capitalistic charlatanry links general contention with success. This is a deeply psychologically problem that simply does not exist in most African, Asian, and South American countries.

Claiming that Westerner's problems are unimportant because more materially deprived people living in poorer countries is incredible, well, materialistic. Of course, people living in the First World have issues unique to living in the First World. Depression and anxiety are two problems that might even characterise Western life, for instance. All things considered, it might be most appropriate to narrow the regional problems down into awfully yet attractively reductionist statements.

- The people of the 'West's problems are typically psychological.
- The people of the 'Rest's' problems are typically physiological.

Feel No Shame, You King

There is no shame in being materialistic in a materialistic realm, despite the negative connotations of such a personality trait and value. In order to be happy, most people need to do what they need to do. Therefore, it is not immoral to take shortcuts to success, provided they do not harm others. Sure, some might see one as a Machiavellian-piece-of-something, but the means do not always require justification. Only through the material can one gain the respect of the materialist, and the materialists are the most influential figure in society. However, once one has this attention and power, they can do with it what they will.

Materialism is not always evil. 'Good' materialism voices that material artefacts can serve a higher educational or religious purpose. Specifically, God Himself came in three forms: The Father, The Son, and The Holy Spirit. One of His forms was material flesh, Jesus Christ. So, Christianity teaches us that, through the material body, one can also reach the arcane.

Additionally, physical possessions can represent sacred meaning to individuals and will positively influence their behaviour. In the arts, for example, one might be affected by legendary renaissance art and culture in such a way that utterly transforms their moral paradigm, or a winner of an award might experience feelings of personal accomplishment. Therefore, it is important to remember that material objects can serve a good purpose if one chooses to do so.

As a rule, people must never base their entire self-image on material things, in any case. Thus, for example, if a person is poor, they might feel worthless as they own little value in material goods; if they are rich, they might feel pretentious as they own much in material goods. Thus, by the material, one can find callousness and greed, but also charity and sympathy.

It is not what one possesses, but what they do with their possessions, that matters.

Chapter Eight: Socialisation

Defining Socialisation

Socialisation is a part of what makes up the interconnecting 'social order' of a functionalist society (see *Chapter Eleven*) by the behaviourist way of either classical or operant conditioning. It is the process of learning the shared norms and values of society in order for people to know how to behave in a manner that helps them conform to fortify social unity and could also be regarded as a form of social control. Thus, for example, children are taught to believe that hurting others is wrong. Therefore, they will be unlikely to commit violent acts of crime in the future. So, after being socialised, people should theoretically all be able to live perfect lives as good-little citizens, because should someone fall out of line with the social order, then they will only have themselves to blame.

Relevant to both sociology and developmental psychology, two basic methods of socialisation occur during childhood: primary and secondary. Primary socialisation occurs in the household whereby children are taught practical social etiquette, whereas secondary socialisation functions to internalise society's ideologies more theoretically. Either way, both social learning methods strive for the same ultimate goal: to prevent social deviance.

Primary Socialisation: Introduction

Children are not born into the world with an intrinsic understanding of social etiquette. Thus, they learn the correct ways to behave from their immediate environment. Primarily, this social learning occurs within a child's family household, where they emotionally, socially, and intellectually develop from the behaviours, mannerisms, and teachings of their primary social group through direct observation. The branch of informal education, known as primary socialisation, will cement the foundation of the infant's values throughout their life into the adult years, so, to ensure that their values are constructed in a way that allows them to build relationships with themselves and others, their values must be solid and functional with society.

Whether they are taught with respect to the shared values of society or not, family values are the ultimate product of primary socialisation. As children learn from their home, they begin to see the world through the lenses of their parents (or guardians); children's tendency to feel love, hate, and all things between will be biased per the perception of their parents' moral code. The mysticism of the mind concurs that a child's inherited moral code will influence their behaviours, ideologies, and thought processes for as long as they live; even if a person wishes to progressively shift their biased conscious mindset later in life, the sheer length of time that they have spent controlled by a learned morality warrants that they will be eternally poisoned by their unconscious. For example, Freud, referring to it as the 'superego', theorised that the human moral code is formed in a child's first five years as they unconsciously internalise their parents' moral standards in response to approval and punishment.

Essentially, what a child learns from their parents will stay with them for the rest of their life. Therefore, it is of the utmost importance that the child's parents are careful and considerate with what they teach.

Primary Socialisation: Radicalisation

Whilst radicalisation can occur in various scenarios entertaining extremism, children are especially vulnerable to radicalisation at the hands of parents with strong ideological views due to their natural suggestibility. To illustrate, imagine a financially privileged child with vain, classist parents: their personality is likely that of a snobbish kind, and they will probably view the working-class as of lesser importance, even stigmatising them as lazy, stupid, and unclean. Consequently, the child radicalised into the bowls of extremist classism will be conditioned to develop antisocial and prejudiced attitudes against people living in poverty, but not all radicalised children as classists, extremist children include, yet are not limited to, racists, fascists, homophobes, sexists, ableists, ageists, and xenophobes who may still hold prejudice against multiple social groups solely due to their irresponsibly ignorant upbringing.

Radicalised children are not condemned to be extremists for the rest of their lives, but since their conditioning has imbued belligerence within the very roots of their subconscious, they will always be affected by what they were forced to learn.

Primary Socialisation: Models of Parenthood

Different styles of parenting will lead to different outcomes in primary socialisation. For example, assertive parents will usually socialise a greater level of self-discipline in their children, whereas parents who are lenient with their child's own freedom to express themselves might socialise them to feel a greater degree of pride. However, no parenting styles are without their flaws: rewarding children too frequently can lead to the development of narcissistic personality disorder (NPD), just as shouting at children, irrespective of the correctness of their behaviour, causes a double-bind dilemma in communication whereby a child learns an inability to respond to stimuli correctly and will potentially develop schizophrenia. Moreover, concerning self-expression, left-wing Westerners characteristically condemn children's indoctrination whilst simultaneously pressuring parents to encourage them to explore their inherent individuality. This vehemently liberal leftist nativity deprives children of the West of the guidance they need to make informed decisions, meaning that more liberal parents will gleefully sacrifice their children's need for the orderly guardianship critical to support them in making informed decisions for an ironically religious measure of social conformity that neglects their best interests. In contrast, right-wing families often disregard the opinions and wishes of their children to fortify the importance of orderly rules for behaviour and combat chaotic attitudes, hence why any and all models of parenthood will surely conjure some negative outcomes.

There is no such thing as 'bad' parenting, despite what anyone unfortunate enough to dwell in the Western cesspool of grandiose delusions will say. Whether one has grown up in a nuclear family or a 'broken' one, all mainstream parenting styles have their own advantages and disadvantages, therefore to judge one another for their upbringing is to follow the Western path of the exceedingly clueless yet ever so common idiot. Parents are largely responsible for their child's moral code, but they are not the only contributing factor.

Secondary Socialisation: Introduction

Other than within their household, children are also educated on societal norms at school. Since an 1880 amendment to the 1870 Education Act, school attendance has been compulsory in some areas of Europe to ensure that children pass through some kind of educational system, whether it be to either conform to the will of governmental authorities, to be prepared for occupational life, or to simply be gifted an academic education of life and all of its wonders.

Today, academic education in the West is usually split into three distinctive categories: primary, secondary, and tertiary. Primary and secondary education systems typically provide a fixed curriculum, with secondary education offering a more advanced level of learning than those aged up to eleven years old studying numeracy and literacy in primary school. Tertiary education, however, is an entire path whereby a student can choose a specific theoretical discipline that they have previously succeeded in to develop an 'expertise' in pursuit of a career. Overall, all tiers of academia seek to educate pupils at a level that corresponds to their age and aptitude whilst motivating the conjuration of an ultimate goal in individuals in line with a subject that they succeed in.

Secondary Socialisation: Academia and Structural Functionalism

Measuring and ranking aptitude is pivot to the functional aspect of the Western education systems. For example, students will have their exams numerically marked in line with listed criteria and will be provided with a grade relevant to how accurately their answers conformed to that criteria. Perhaps this is another form of socialisation in itself, to learn the competitive nature of society that assures the 'best' will be placed above the 'rest', who must passively accept the harsh reality that their inability is the reason for their lowly position, rather than crying out scapegoating accusations of systematic oppression. Unsurprisingly, students who achieve below-average grades are likely to suffer from low self-esteem as a consequence of how they are made to feel solely responsible for their lack of academic success.

It is not in the interests of Western academia to nurture an authentic connection between a student and a subject of their choosing any more than it is to force one between the students and a subject of the establishment's choosing. To elaborate, students are not free to explore subjects of their complete choice in the UK as schools do not have a wide range of subjects on their curriculum. Take the humanities, for example. As the spotlights shift to highlight the sciences as the most prominent due to the popularity of materialism, the need for a cultured understanding of the arts is lessened in society. Therefore, students are deprived of the opportunity for wider reading because society sees little to no importance in the subject matter, irrespective of the student's individual values. Moreover, this narrow-minded practical limitation sees that students are not supported in making more informed decisions in certain life scenarios:

    1. Since languages are not compulsory, the volume of monolingualism is bound to increase in English-speaking countries, perhaps to fortify international or racial segregation.

    2. Since religious studies are not compulsory, the volume of religious hate crime is bound to at least stay the same in countries where religious intolerance is already strong, perhaps to fortify religious segregation.

    3. Since students are not taught how to manage their money, the volume of people living in poverty is bound to at least stay the same in economically disadvantaged regions, perhaps to fortify the difficulty of social mobility.

Simply put, academia functions to socialise children in social conformity so that they do not escape societal oppression.

Secondary Socialisation: Bullying, Cliques, and Isolation

A highly specific yet telling point highlighting how students doubt themselves, feel ostracised, and underachieve across Western academia is its use of 'gifted and talented' groups.

Up until recently, students were sat down to undertake a cognitive ability test with the purpose of measuring their aptitude for learning through assessment of their reasoning skills. The test was taken at the very beginning of year seven and provided students with their predicted grades for the entirety of key stage 3, irrespective of the actual grades they received in individual subjects. This meant that the school itself valued intelligence over aptitude for a particular area of study, in addition to students' behaviour and effort. As a result of this ignorance, non-gifted pupils that were doing better than gifted pupils on an academic level had their success undermined as they were still predicted to do worse than the lucky few despite their higher grades. Additionally, this reduced the incentive to drive both sets of students to work harder in order to achieve their goals as the non-gifted students are not sufficiently rewarded for doing well, and the gifted students are essentially being told that because they possess a higher ability to learn, they will simply learn at a better rate than others anyway and achieve higher grades than the non-gifted students independent of how hard they try. This could also explain the brief surge in average student wellbeing since the abolishment of the programme.

Whilst testing the cognitive abilities of primary school students via IQ tests is uncommon in the UK, such practices in other first-world countries do occur, like in the USA. The common causes of selecting the 'smartest' minority of young pupils and treating them differently to other pupils to this extent have, in most cases, concluded with the isolation of those gifted pupils more than any other. This is due to a number of reasons: children of this age can be especially cruel and will likely be envious of the gifted few - resulting in bullying and juvenile name-calling (e.g. "nerd"); the gifted pupils will themselves become overly proud of the newly achieved status bestowed upon them and ridicule others for not being as clever as them; a gifted child can become constantly aware of the failure and develop strong anxiety at a very young age.

As so many gifted students put so much importance on the concept of going to University and getting a degree, it is common for them to crack under their own pressure. Many former-gifted pupils do not attend tertiary education until they are mature students, if they attend at all. This is as opposed to the fact that the average IQ of university students in Western society (who had completed what is equivalent to at least a UK level 5 qualification) is 104, which is well within the common average bracket of 91-109, which means one's ability to enter a university is not really relative to their intelligence. Therefore, the pressure gifted students place on themselves to achieve this, because of the nature of the gifted and talented programme in secondary school, is entirely misplaced. This is also a major reason for the popularity of the contemporary phenomenon 'gifted-kid burnout', which is self-explanatory.

The lack of virtue displayed by Western education systems is apparent through analysis of their use of their precious elitist programmes in which they use the members to showcase what the establishment itself is achieving (a word used very loosely), rather than performing their duty of care by safely nurturing young people academically. For example, as a member of this group, Ashley Dymond would be a part of both regional and national competitions where students at different schools would compete against each other. Obviously, the winners of these competitions would be the schools themselves, fortifying his claim that schools use these pupils as pawns in an effort to establish their own superiority, instead of looking after the wellbeing of these pupils and assisting them on their journey in using their 'gifts' to become valuable members of society.

Secondary Socialisation: Anti-Intellectual Academia

There is a sense of equity missing in Western academia. Students from all backgrounds need to be told that high grades are not unobtainable, and the students getting better grades than them are no more naturally competent; subjects are all knowledge-based, so, with encouragement and support, anyone can study hard enough to do well.

Academia, especially within tertiary education, is permeated with pre-expectations of students to wear their political biases upon their shoulders as, should they not, students will be harassed and bullied for taking a moral 'inaction' by omniscient pink-haired philanthropists (wow, just look at those readings on the sarcasm detector). Of course, being bullied will lower a student's self-esteem and their motivation to achieve high grades will fall, but being bullied simply for refusing to conform to the normalised views of the classroom is malevolently anti-intellectual. Academia should remain objective, keeping informal subjectivity out of the classroom. School children are socialised to hold overzealous beliefs that there are Nazis behind every corner; the education system contorts them into delusional freaks. Even in tertiary education, a 'resisting whiteness' conference held at the University of Edinburgh attempted to plague Scotland with a racist ideology that the undefined characteristics of the collective white-man are evil, a catastrophically polarising and embarrassingly example of idiotic lunacy. Rather than promoting the learning of objective truths, the Western, postmodernist education system now only seeks to maintain an infantile denial of reality.

In further attempting to cement a culture of political correctness, education establishments will sanitise history, so to speak. For example, excerpts from 'Huckleberry Finn' are largely censored for having racial themes, despite the fact that these themes were used to illustrate how outrageous racial discrimination is and to promote civil equality. The representation of moral ambiguities that academia hates so much is essential in comprehending how to diminish social issues. Even children understand this. Depicting acts of racism is not racism; it is myopic to purge the past where things offend us now. Consequently, the Western oversimplification of moral issues deprives people of education, leaving them dumb to social issues. Today, people can claim discrimination wherever they want.

Marcus Aurelius once said, "everything we hear is an opinion, not a fact. Everything we see us a perspective, not the truth." This has been mistakenly adopted by postmodernists as authoritative support for their ideology. However, Aurelius spoke of how truths are twisted by individual interpretations and biases rather than the utter absence of objective fact.

All information previously learned at universities can now be learned online. So, in order to become educated, one must educate oneself wherever one can.

"We become what we know", Søren Kierkegaard.

Be careful what you know.

Chapter Nine: Occupations

The Good and Bad of Work-Life

Since Western education systems see that completion of at least the secondary-level is compulsory, students are (usually) gifted with the choice of using their qualifications for either an entry-level job in a field of their choice where they can work their way up into illustrious and well-paid trade management with vocational qualifications or for admission into tertiary education where they can study their chosen theoretical discipline across the heights of academia, before combining their studies with practical experience to demonstrate the sufficient competence required to kick start their professional careers in the big-wide-world. Given that both of these paths into occupational life, in most areas, provide those taking them with a steady income, pride, and the potential to make like-minded friends, the pitiful idealist could be excused for assuming that the entirety of the West, rather than just the USA, housed the 'land of opportunity'. Yet, in the harsh and merciless reality of the West, people who do not inherit assets or professional shortcuts might find themselves overworked for little pay in an endless pursuit of a career that provides them with just enough to live out the weakest versions of their dreams temporarily. In the UK, the average university graduate fails to obtain a graduate-level role, just as the lifelong tradesman endures years of demotivation in their longing for a promotion that ultimately renders them content to settle for line management at best. Still, these people are the lucky ones. Should one delve into the very depths of the working-class (due to disagreement in how to define social classes, the phrase 'working-class' refers to labourers, in this text), they shall find a minimum-wage job, or even beneficiary dependent individuals who entertain no element of a social life outside of their places for economic 'survival'.

To expand on how occupational life negatively affects the emotional, financial, and social welfare of the working-class, people who work minimum-wage jobs are also often stuck in them. Sometimes, this is because they are denied opportunities for promotion. Other times, it is because they do not feel worthy of promotion. Either way, the root of the problem stays the same; working-class people are negatively stigmatised as foolish failures who frequently engage in self-destructive behaviours which are responsible for the lowly position that they are in, such as drug abuse or violent crime. Thus, they are seen as untrustworthy, both by others and themselves. This undesirable image forced upon the economically oppressed (or the lazy) is a reason for their dissatisfaction with their current work life. For example, a janitor is ridiculed and earns little pay for their work which causes them to effectively hate their job, yet they also cannot simply leave as they would only work another minimum-wage job and run into the same problems. The janitor, and any other labourers, will therefore be vulnerable to suffering from mental health issues consequent of their depleting self-images.

Social Approval

Humans are social creatures; it is only human nature to crave social approval. Social respect even underpins human ambition. Interestingly, depending on whom one asks, humans have either been socialised or have evolved to seek out material accomplishment and hierarchal social dominance, thus motivating people to work to achieve these things. Although, if a person's good performances are ignored and go unrewarded, they can become even more motivated to work harder and perform better, assuming that they are fortuitous in their willpower and character. Though, should a person be extremely sensitive and insecure, they might become bitter become angry at an apparently unjust world when they are denied immediate gratification for their actions, even growing a terribly intense resentment of their bosses.

In order to obtain social approval, humans conjure particular self-images of themselves that they wish others to see them as. To main this desired perception, one must never appear to behave in a manner that is inconsistent with their image. However, when the normative values of society inevitably clash with those of the self, one cannot possibly act in a way that will both appear unfoolish and respectful to their own essence.

Perhaps fiercer than the human need for social approval is the need for self-approval. This is a simple yet powerful thing to understand, but accepting and loving oneself is not so easy as simply building up self-esteem. In order to truly accept oneself, one must be willing to change their beliefs when one is proven wrong, for if they are not so humbly willing, then their omniscient unconscious will recognise when one lies to themselves to maintain their fallacious beliefs, as one is what they believe. If one can only bear to change their incorrect beliefs just enough so as not to have to accept the truth, then they are using cognitive dissonance, a cognition that helps people to change their beliefs when proven wrong without facing up to the truth. For example, say a situation arises that makes a subject appear silly, this person might alter their belief so as not to appear irrational but instead as rational and consistent as, otherwise, they would not be able to cope with their lack of self-approval. This is a method used by people with fragile egos to protect them from the pain of accepting their own irrationality. Of course, should a person take the decision to accept their own irrationality, there will still be emotional effects, but they will be worth it in the bigger picture. In the short term, a person might develop lower self-esteem after acknowledging that they were wrong, especially if they held their prior beliefs dear. Likewise, this person will also suffer a long-term effect by potentially being affected by the bad memory later in life. However, by their decision to accept the truth, they will not be plagued by a lie or be subjected to live a life dissociative from reality.

The Police, Public Opinion, and Stanley Milgram

The public opinion on morally ambiguous companies can often mean that people working for these companies are characterised as evil, despite the inherent invalidity of such an overreaching assumption. To clear up this topic, Stanley Milgram, an American psychologist, conducted a study of obedience that seeks to explain why good people do bad things, especially in the workplace.

In italics below is an extract, concerning Milgram, of a first-class essay on 'Key Studies in Psychology' that the author wrote in his first year at university:

Between 1961-1963, American Psychologist Stanley Milgram conducted a series of experiments at Yale University and Bridgeport inspired by the Nuremberg trials. Consequently, Milgram gathered 540 local volunteers (500 male; 40 female) and two actors to participate in his "Study of Learning", aiming to test the length to which people will go to obey an instruction from an authority figure and to investigate the circumstances under which that person would obey them. Regarding equipment, Milgram used a fake but fatal looking and sounding "deluxe volt generator" to convince participants of the experiment's reality upon Mr William's (acting authority figure) introduction to it and Mr Wallace (acting learner). Afterwards, a rigged lottery was drawn to delegate the participant to the "teacher" role, whereby they would test the learner's memory after they had been strapped into a chair and connected to the generator. Upon every incorrect answer, the participant was instructed to electrocute Wallace with increasing voltage capped at 450V, which would determine their obedience. This experiment resulted in a sixty-five per cent rate of obedience, whereas when Williams instructed via phone, it dropped to twenty per cent, and a further ten per cent when the learner was accompanied by two rebellious learners. Milgram concluded an extreme willingness in authoritative obedience that was dispositional and situational and theorised the "agentic shift" as a cause for this (McLeod, 2017).

Milgram's experiment possessed a reliable experimental design (Benjamin & Simpson, 2009). For example, his independent variable of pressure and the dependent variable of obedience presented a clear cause and effect relationship as generally, with less authoritative pressure came less obedience. Consequently, the experimental research can be easily replicated and tested. Additionally, Milgram retained high experimental realism as when questioning participants on how authentic they felt Williams' pain was in a follow-up study, they answered an average of 13.4/14, thus supporting the notion that participants were successfully immersed in the experiment (Benjamin & Simpson, 2009). However, the experiment lacked ecological validity due to the unrealistic situations studied in the laboratory setting, such as the operation of a volt generator (Perry, 2013). Therefore, without considering secondary research support, Milgram's findings cannot be used to explain events occurring in lesser controlled environments. Furthermore, the experiments partially lacked theoretical value. To expand, Milgram neglects to consider the possibility of obedience influences other than authoritative pressure. So, his research loses validity, perhaps due to researcher bias as he wanted to study authority (Perry, 2013). Ethical responsibility issues also arise when analysing Milgram's research as three participants suffered seizures during the experiments, thus indicating Milgram's negligence in participant protection during the experiment, despite subsequent participant debriefings and check-ups (Milgram, 1963).

Milgram's theory of the agentic state inspired many psychologists, like Hofling, Zimbardo, and Burger, to conduct research into situations whereby a subject may look to shift the responsibility of executing a morally questionable action to another agent. Furthermore, conclusions drawn from these studies often supported that of Milgram. Therefore, Milgram's research can be interpreted as revolutionary (Grzyb, et al., 2017).

Conceivably, Milgram's reliable theory of the 'agentic state' neatly explains that people who perform immoral acts in their job justify their behaviour as they are following instructions from commanding, authoritative figures.

Today, police in France, Spain, the UK, and the USA have been called to be 'defunded' by mobs of left-wing protesters, citing their reason as the problems of police brutality and racial profiling. Obviously, such violence and unequal treatment are problematic, irrespective of the cause, so their reasons are justified. However, it is when these protests radicalise people into hating police officers as individuals that civil injustice occurs. Much like how one should condemn the ideology rather than the ideologist, people should never have their morality measured by their occupation, for it will only ever serve to destroy empathy, inclusion, and logic.

The Alignment of Goals and Values

In order to live an authentic and fulfilling life, it is essential that one aligns their goals with their values. If they fail to do this, one will surely despair, even putting themselves at risk of an existential crisis after years of pursuit of uninspired, normalised goals cause them to dwell over the lack of meaning that they have infused into their own life. Strangely, this existentialist theory is mirrored in the gospel of Matthew, with the story of Judas and his betrayal of the Messiah. Judas Iscariot, a materialistic disciple of Jesus Christ, cursed with earthly desires, betrayed the holy Son of God for thirty pieces of silver after he kissed Him on the cheek and publicly addressed Him as 'Rabbi'. After learning that Christ was to be crucified by the Romans, Judas could not forgive himself. Thus, he could not bring himself to repent. Instead, unable to believe that Jesus would have forgiven him at His resurrection, he desperately tried to return the valueless silver before committing suicide in Hakeldama. Today, people can look to Judas and see a man whose values of devotion, faith, and love, as taught to him through Christ, were not compatible with his materialistic goals. Therefore, his life was ruined.

To correctly align their goals and values, one should ensure that they are following a career path that they feel deeply and personally connected to; one should ask themselves: "do I feel proud?", "will I reflect on this with pride?" and "does my occupation help me to do 'good', as I understand 'good'?".

A happy man is a man who is happy with his place in the world and how it contributes to a purpose bigger than himself.

Chapter Ten: Liberty

What is Liberty?

The word 'liberty' refers to the state of individual independence of legislative restrictions that are deemed 'oppressive'. In the Middle East, for example, many societies are governed by totalitarian state leaders who outlaw the act of speaking out against their dictatorship, which they might make punishable by death. The Western world, however, is notably more liberal, evidenced by its legislation. For instance, the United States is founded upon constitutional rights in the form of amendments, whereby the initial ten make up the 'Bill of Rights' that was inspired by third U.S. president Thomas Jefferson, earning the U.S. the nickname of 'Land of the Free', which was also inspired following the declaration of independence from the British empire in the eighteenth century. Additionally, members of the European Union (E.U.), among other sovereign states, were granted a 'European Convention on Human Rights' (ECHR), effective from 1953, from the Council of Europe, based in Strasbourg. Later, Tony Blair's 'new labour' incorporated the convention into British law through the introduction of the 'Human Rights Act 1998', which, in its fifth article, states that are British citizens must have their human right to liberty and security respected by others and the state. Overall, liberal freedoms and rights are flagships of Western democracies.

Democracy and Individual Liberty

Western countries are democratic states, meaning that the people in these countries hold power to elect political leaders. Democracies usually come in four forms: constitutional, direct, monitory, and representative, though their core principle remains the same. To some, like Jefferson, democracies are necessary to ensure that the values of the people are maintained by its government and their civic rights are protected from tyrannies. To others, like Socrates, democracies naively trusts their citizenries to make decisions that they are unqualified to make, causing chaotic, dysfunctional, and unsafe societies. Interestingly, more contemporary critics claim that democratic governments paint illusions of liberal democracy to blind the people to the tyrannical volumes of social control that surround them. For example, during a parliamentary election, also known as a general election, the U.K.'s supposedly democratic order convinces people that they are voted for whom they want on their own accord, but in reality, their choice has been biased as they are pitted against each other by campaigners who demonise both ideologies and ideologists, and they become but a sheep in the herd. Thus, the radicalisation inherent in Western democracies that so easily puppeteer their unaware populations leads to extremism, and extremists are driven by hatred rather than free will, according to the corresponding social critics.

'Individual liberty' can be defined as the personal freedom to do as one pleases, should not impose on the rights of others. It is also one of four 'fundamental British values' along with 'democracy', 'rule of law', and 'respect and tolerance'. As explained before, liberty is a conventional human right. It profoundly establishes equality, where it is effective, through the equal protection of every citizen's rights, irrespective of their membership of any social group. However, equality is not equity; it is through the absolutist equal treatment that the ECHR ignores the social barriers to liberty that members of different social groups are vulnerable to face, destroying the possibility of social diversity in these societies that are too riddled with discrimination to break glass ceilings and see every social group represented in every stage of organisational hierarchies. Sure, parliament may have passed the Equality Act 2010 in an effort to combat discrimination towards nine social groups listed in the legislation as 'protected characteristics', but fails to recognise that British society is made up of more than nine social groups, perhaps even inflicting further social isolation and vulnerability upon those left unprotected, such as the working-class.

To generalise, the stark obstacles barring specific social groups from perceivably selective life opportunities is an indication of the illiberalism of liberal democracies. As is made apparent by the informed claims of academic sociologists, socioeconomic mobility is rarely observed in British culture. Therefore, the working-class have been deprived of the tools of liberty, for their overwhelming majority have not used them to grow. Do they simply choose not to? Are they all just stupid? The mind boggles...

To see another case of inequitable distribution of liberty, one might look to the cultural assimilation of immigrants in the United States. Whilst there can be no claims of multicultural representation in federal policy, many Americans suggest that their country is multicultural; as a matter of fact, Republicans are thought to claim that "good ol' USA" is too multicultural and that they have lost a sense of national identity due to mass immigration. Given, America may have built a few Mosques here and there to accommodate a handful of Muslims, but it cannot be classified as a multicultural society. In order for multiculturalism to be present, society requires that no overarching tyrannical constructs are present in their culture. Naturally, these constructs are present in the USA by way of Christianity. Despite founding the country upon secular constitutions of law, the star-spangled bureaucrats based their actual laws on Judeo-Christian values, a statement made at the risk of sounding like just another Jordan Peterson wannabe. This means that there is an American culture that migrants must ultimately assimilate to rather than integrate with if they wish to become functional members of society. Thus, say, devout Hindus must not have the liberty to be culturally deviant from the shared values of an incompatible society, as Hinduism as incompatible with Christianity and Judaism.

The Discrimination Problem

Across the West, there lies a constant law, albeit legislated in different ways. Americans might call it freedom of speech, Europeans might call it freedom of expression, but its core principle remains the same: a person has the right to relay their personal beliefs to whomever they see fit, free of punishment, provided that they do not impede on the other party's own rights. Staggeringly, unevolved libertarians routinely excuse prejudiced behaviour via worship of free speech, failing miserably to comprehend that discrimination is still illegal. Although, such cases highlight the dangers of individual liberties like free speech because their vagueness leads to either a definite misinterpretation of the law or a court case riddled with subjectivity. To paint a bigger picture, imagine you have attempted to joke with a Muslim for their use of a turban, a stupid but innocent gesture of playful teasing, and they have taken great offence to it. In the U.K., there is no way of empirically measuring, or better yet, proving whether or not discrimination has occurred. Not by the Human

Rights Act 1998, not by the Communications Act 2003, and not by the Equality Act 2010. No act of parliament has established a method of proving whether or not discrimination has occurred. Whilst this causes clear criminological problems, it should be obvious anyway. How can you prove whether something said was offensive? Nothing is universally offensive. Therefore, nothing is objectively offensive. The Muslim may not have liked to joke, but in order to incriminate a person for saying it, it must be proven that there was malicious intent, something that is entirely unaccountable and subjective. Due to this methodological and theoretical limitation in convicting somebody for discriminatory harassment by charges of hate speech, many innocent people have been wrongfully convicted and lost life opportunities as a ridiculous consequence. Even then, the defendants might win the case but still be found to have been perceived to be offensive by the accuser, meaning that they have still committed non-crime hate speech against one of now five protected characteristics, in this case, this is religion, which affects their chances of getting a job, for instance, as it the non-crime incident will appear on a DBS check. Unfortunately, the only way for society to scale this issue is for people to simply 'toughen up', maintain personal resilience, and allow jokes, as 'savage' as they may be, to be just that, jokes. Cruel or not, this is the only way.

The Dangers of Liberty: Excessive Rights

As it stands, free speech does threaten the majority of the West, for how could such a weak-minded, tribalistic society resist being offended? Consequently, they cannot be deemed to have been granted the liberty to feel self-esteem as Westerners are socialised into emotionally sensitive, segregated tribes in a heavily polarised and venomous culture war. On account of this, members of civilisations with constitutional protection for free speech often use their freedoms to maliciously demoralise people that they do not like. For example, a student of Asian ethnicity may not like another student of African-American ethnicity, and they might mock them in a number of ways but pretend that they are joking. Due to the first amendment, 'merica enables the bigots of its citizenry to prejudice and escape punishment, meaning that victims of verbal prejudice cannot do anything but absorb the abuse.

British conservatives have, somewhat predictably, condemned the Human Rights Act 1998 for gifting excessive rights to British citizens. In 2005, to elaborate, a student was allowed back into school after committing arson on school grounds, with respect to their 'right to education'. Critics understandably lambasted this decision as the arsonist posed a claim danger to the staff and other students at the school, but, because of the Western tendency to be excessively liberal when delegating rights across its democracies, individual liberty trumped the collective's best interests once again.

The Dangers of Liberty: The COVID-19 Pandemic

As of June 2021, COVID-19 has killed almost four million people worldwide. So, in order to save lives, the world health organisation has worked with world leaders and scientists to develop and distribute vaccinations that will prevent more deaths. The libertarian geniuses, however, make brilliant use of their liberty, refusing to save lives. Wonderful! One wonders, what philosophical reason could they have for such drastic action? Here are some hysterical highlights…

- "Coronavirus only kills less than 1% [3,900,000] of the people it infects."
- "COVID-19 is no worse than the common cold."

- "It is a violation of my human rights [that I have no idea why I'm exercising]!"
- "Vaccines cause autism."
- "Vaccines might cause a zombie apocalypse."

Ironically, should these people actually grow a brain cell and get vaccinated, then social distancing restrictions would be lifted quicker. Thus, they are literally preventing liberty by exercising their liberal right to protest.

Liberty and Social Control

On a more serious note, and to be blunt, with the volume of surveillance permeating Western society today, free will might as well be considered an illusion.

Western governments spit in the face of liberty for the glory of social control. Across the shops and streets of a town square, for example, governments demonstrate such a lack of trust in their own people that they must watch their every move through CCTV cameras, smearing society in a sea of video surveillance. Note that, should they take a misstep, individuals will be immediately punished by the omnipotent, omnipresent, and the omniscient rule of law. For all its justifiable purpose, how can such an almighty society even grant liberty when its people are too scared to even be perceived to step out of line?

P.S.: Do try not to accept digital cookies from strangers.

Disgusting, Terrifying Freedom

According to existentialist Jean-Paul Sartre, every dweller of a capitalist nation is cursed with freedom because they are responsible for every failure that they endure. Sartre views on Western freedom were influenced by nineteenth-century Danish theologian Søren Kierkegaard, who was dubbed the father of existentialism. On individual liberty, he said that humans all desire freedom of social constraints, however, these same conceptual freedoms is terrifying to the individual. On offering a solution to this angst, Kierkegaard proposed that one must develop and complete faith in themselves and in God, thus becoming a 'knight of faith'. This way, one could overcome the oppressive nature of society's bestowed liberty and obtain real, authentic freedom.

Both in ignorance and spite of their individual freedoms, Westerners seem to really hate their lives. Why, though? Maybe people are just attracted to dystopian views. Dostoevsky even pointed out that people who appreciate the world and are grateful for their existence are labelled idiots as they are perceived to not be able to comprehend the oppression surrounding them, especially in the view of Marxists, who think that life's flaws must always kill a wise man's livelihood. Critically, these critics fail to understand that, even in the face of tragedy, happiness is can always be found, provided one is wise enough to see it. For example, should one unequivocally refuse to live in fear and resentment but instead snatch at their freedom to feel gratitude for what they have, then they will find joy in their existence. By this, the Russian novelist urged his readers to become enchanted by the beauty of life, a life that is not perfect, but one that can be imbued with such glorious purpose, should they freely choose it to be meaningful.

Chapter Eleven: Social Order

Functionalism

Before we dive into an analysis of the social constructs that keep the cogs of our society turning, let us look to the source of these fundamental forces at play, functionalism.

Functionalism, or structural functionalism, is a sociological theory that concurs that the survival of society is dependent on the existence of order, order that can only exist if the structure of society functions to cement it. The functionalist claims that an orderly society is beneficial to both the organisations and individuals that comprise it as order prompts people to work together and help each other; order encourages economic growth and social connection, which both enable society to grow in power and unity. Therefore, a rich and content society would behold the ability to achieve its governing body's noble goals absent of the potential interference of social uprisings.

The functionalist perspective is mostly interested in Western society since the nineteenth century, or more specifically, since industrialisation. In the events of the birth of new technological advances, production rates of material goods would skyrocket, and a plethora of new occupational opportunities arose for commoners across the land. According to the functionalist, society had escaped the unchivalrous chains of feudalism and transitioned into a new world, an equal opportune world bare of landowners spitting on helpless peasants, a world where anyone could achieve the riches of their wildest dreams, a world... of capitalism.

Ideally, in the capitalist socioeconomic system, dreams could become a reality. Capitalism provided hope with the championing of the importance of the nation-state, liberty, and individual growth. However, for people to serve and strive for these goals, changes had to be made. The nuclear family became popularised, and gender roles were implored, allowing for effective use of the public and private spheres; the husband could focus on making money for his family without the hassle of childcare and household chores as his faithful housewife would be at home taking care of the domestic duties that all 'good wives' should. Furthermore, the importance of family values diminished in favour of communal servitude, creating greater loyalty to the region, hence society.

Shockingly(!), functionalism is often criticised for a capitalist bias. As shall soon be explored, it possesses a tendency to justify the tyrannical nature of society's departments by exclaiming that the functions they perform are key to the survival of society itself, thus, the welfare of the humans encompassing it. As Marx claims, the bourgeoisie (the dominant class in capitalist societies) would financially oppress the proletariats (the oppressed class in capitalist societies), who only had their unskilled work of value, through low-paid, long-hour manual labour. Yet, the proletariats would be passive to this oppression surrounding them due to the social constructs and services available, like 'the opium of the people' religion and working man leisurely distractions from social justice unions like football. Meanwhile, Weber argued that capitalism was not tolerated because of religion. Rather it was a child of Calvinism where individual accountability to demonstrate benevolence with riches. It sounds explicable capitalist, does it not? So, how could discussing society through the lens of such a tainted theory be useful in explaining how it really impacts the psychological wellbeing of its citizenry? Well, by adopting the functionalist perspective to analyse the functions of the components within society, we access an extremely ecologically valid reasoning for these concepts as they only exist because of functionalism, so what best way to explain them? Additionally, functionalism holds a capitalist bias, and we still live in a capitalist society. Therefore, functionalism provides the most idealistic opinion, so should there be inconsistencies with the functionalist's expectations on social behaviour and reality, we would know then that capitalism cannot be truly functional.

Social Order

We have established that society is composed of different elements that perform different functions, but what are they and what do they do? Social order is split into six sections: *cooperation* – society working together to achieve common goals, *social unity* – society conforming to a set of criteria, *shared norms* – shared societal guides for behaviour, *shared values* – shared societal beliefs about what is important, *socialisation* – the process of learning culture in society, *social control* – societal mechanisms that encourage the acceptance of conformity. These elements complement one another to ensure passive adherence to society's desires. From dress codes to the criminal justice system, society uses everything to tighten its grip on order by maintaining the status quo.

Society is sometimes thought of as a system like the human body with different organisations acting as organs, performing a variety of services that allow the human body to happily and healthily function. This is called the organic metaphor. To elaborate, society has many social constructs proving imperative to the survival of social order: sport, hospitals, shops, transport, to name a few. Likewise, the human body's organs maintain the survival of the individual, which is possible because of the orderly functions of the body. In a system deprived of these functional elements, the system would break and become chaotic. This chaos causes systems to become hostile areas; think an anarchical uprising leading to a mass killing or a human without a heart pumping blood around the body. As the system would not be able to function as designed, a range of unpredictable effects could result, such as crime, antisocial behaviour, poor physical health, and to a seemingly smaller degree of chaotic consequence, social isolation.

These individuals that fall out of order are undesired, shunned, and cited as an example of what is wrong in society. Yet, they still exist… would they exist in a functional system? Nevertheless, to understand how the social order identifies and isolates the freaks of society, we should examine the different parts of the social order and how they contribute to this problem specifically.

Cooperation

For a society to thrive, everybody needs to help. People need to cooperate to achieve the objectives of their collective group. They need to work together to achieve their common goals, as identified by the social order. Although how does the social order identify these goals and why? The functionalist will tell everyone that it is for the benefit of individual people in society in addition to society as a whole. A system of people may strive to protect each other from violence as their leader's downcast violent acts, but is the system really doing this for the individuals? Obviously, less violence in society protects individuals from physical harm, but it is also lessening the chances of a mass uprising against the oppression within a system, primarily benefitting the system itself and the dominant class. Therefore, a lack of cooperative activity by people would hinder the chance of society reaching its common goals.

The people who do not cooperate in the strive for common goals are labelled as lazy, making society a worse place for everyone in it and relying on others to do all the heavy lifting. This shunning takes place irrespective of individual capacity to cooperate; people do not consider what others can and cannot do for cultural, physical, or emotional barriers. This ignorance is probably the cause of dedication to the collective goals of society and is less likely to be observed in centrists and libertarians who are not extremely emotionally invested in the goals of their society, resultant in blind loyalty. Consequently, there is a higher chance of these people adopting a person-centred approach before judging their collective actions.

The ignorance characterising the expectation for all individuals to contribute towards a common goal is good evidence of our society's inequitable nature. People will be assessed solely for their output, and their values are not considered, watering down the importance of individual expression.

Social Unity

Every weekend, some of us like to get behind our favourite sports teams and cheers them on as they look to triumph in accordance with their grail. Noticeably, all the members of these teams have conformed to specific criterion and dedicate their behaviours to working within them. To unlock social order, society must first establish the criterion, whether outlined in legislation, scripture, or be found in a socially constructed idea via great collective needs, then the devout unit adhering to this criteria can be created. This unit is ideally comprised of everyone within society. Therefore everyone in society is held responsible for their own level of participation. This is social unity.

However, if criteria are not met if a football teams goalkeeper concedes a sloppy goal, all eyes turn to them, even if the overall team performance was poor. If a person dares commit the fatality of an individual error that leads to a key event building up to an undesirable result, then their performance will specifically be highlighted, thus garnering all the blame. This is the major issue with social unity. The unit moral is so integral to its ability and incentive to hold criteria dear that leadership cannot afford to risk demotivating the entire unit. Therefore it focuses on one person to uplift the rest as it was not their fault. Equally, leadership certainly cannot risk enduring any responsibility for the loss themselves, as who follows losers?

Collaterally, the poor performers who are blamed at the expense of the whole social unit are discredited, depriving them of future opportunities to expand their own network and career. Thus, they are isolated as others do not want to be seen working with them; they may even lose friends as a result.

What society can fail to realise is that the unifying criterion simply does not benefit everyone; society does not wave a magic wand to create a set of rules for everyone to adhere to for perfect lives. This criterion is fixed and does not morph to suit individuals meaning that people coming from certain social groups may not be able to play a sufficient role in a unit.

Shared Norms

In an orderly society, correct behaviour is common knowledge. People know what they should and should not be doing as they need only to look around them and observe the actions of everyone else. To see prevalent behaviour within society is to see the unwritten behaviour guides given to specific social groups. These guides outline normal behaviour for people hailing from different groups and help them perform their respective societal functions. For example, within a nuclear family, it is a housewife's role to take care of domestic chores and childhood so the husband can focus on his work, as specified by the normal behaviour of women in marriage. Society needs to share these undisputable ideas of what people should be doing to conform to social order; society is required to believe in shared norms.

Unsurprisingly, if a person acts inconsistently to society's shared idea of their group's social norm, then they can be very quickly identified and ridiculed for being weird. As previously mentioned, the notorious gender norms are a brilliant example of this. Masculine gender norms like leadership and aggression are given to males in society and if a male shows behaviour associated with opposite traits, they are scrutinised for being weak, incapable 'beta-males'. This is the central subject of toxic masculinity, which feminist activists identify as a cause for discrimination and unequal opportunity between sexes as it encourages the petulance of bullying those outside of the norm, hopeful of establishing roles that exclusively benefit men.

Shared norms also limit individuality. They identify a social group and assign designated attitudes and behaviours which collectivise the people within that group by discouraging individual expression.

Shared Values

A value is a belief about what is important or worthwhile. Some may say that the foundation of societal growth is a collective agreement about what material objects or metaphysical concepts are valuable and how valuable they are. Naturally, values shaped goals and rules. Therefore individual behaviour is based on the value that society utilises to form the orderly fashion of society. For example, a random person is found wandering the streets of Derby today is unlikely to be a murder as society declares human life valuable. This is known as a shared value.

Of course, every single person is different and will hold their own set of ideals that they hold value in life, but if any of these values are mutually exclusive to the shared values of society, then this person holding them will become socially isolated and perhaps even feared for untrustworthiness because of our understanding of social order. Just think, we are normally so passive to others being in our personal bubble (at least most of us are) as we un/consciously believe them to share the same values as us, as we are so accustomed to this being the case. Nevertheless, what if someone sat next to someone else at a bus stop wearing a lampshade on their head that read 'my lucky hat'. This object is obviously valuable to them, so much so for them to publicly wear it inexplicably devoid of guilt. Will one feel safe sat next to this individual? One's mind may immediately make assumptions on the danger they might pose and vilify them despite the person being completely innocent. This is because people do not like it when another person does not share the same values as them. We cannot relate to them and may even become ever-more vigilant around them, as society teaches us to do so. On a larger scale, those with certain political values are no less than hated by those who adopt different values. For example, a labour party voter in the UK may view all conservative voters as selfish for the way they vote irrespective of the fact they have no idea of the motivations of the voters other than their perspective of the party as a whole. In 2019, across the Atlantic Ocean to the United States, Ellen DeGeneres, a democrat voter, was substantially condemned for her friendship with George W. Bush, a former Republican US president, as the importance of political leniency is held in such high regard that it overpowers a validity of personal preferences regarding friendship, for much of the public. Obviously, it is intolerance like this that increases social isolation, polarisation and gradually destroys diversity so commonly in the West.

Socialisation

Systems have a phenomenon in place to maintain order. One of these is the way of life for people within a society; from food to sacred ceremonies, culture is everywhere. Now, Western countries tend to have people from many different cultures, hence why they are known as multicultural societies. However, there is always a dominant culture that must be learned. Otherwise, individuals within society will not understand the other components of the social order and will not be tamed, so to speak. The process by which culture is learned is called socialisation.

Since our way of life is never truly static as we (like to think) we are progressing towards shared goals, culture is always changing yet we do not find ourselves having to sit down and read up on our new cultures. Therefore socialisation is surely a passive effect in society. Yet, socialisation blatantly occurs at many different stages...

Primary socialisation refers to the method children learn shared values and norms from their parents, a mother may set domestic chores for her daughter in order to teach her to be a good housewife later in life, or a father may buy his son a toy sword to dogmatise the young one's perception of protectiveness that is so pivotal to the essential gender norms in our functioning society.

Secondary socialisation is an alternative method for the learning process of culture for children where the early-life education system will teach social norms and values. This seems to occur in a variety of different ways, you have the classroom teaching process that is rather straightforward, and you have peer pressure and bullying. If you look around in a classroom, all the cool kids are typically wearing designer brands and have certain hairstyles. These norms are imperative to culture and assert the importance of conformity and self-image at an early age so as to ingrain it into an individual's brain for the rest of their life, regardless of the ethical questions surrounding methods of socialisation like this, society seems to allow it to happen, despite its 'efforts' to prevent bullying with campaigns to raise awareness.

Assimilation is another method of cultural learning for immigrants that are new to their new society's values and norms at a later age. Assimilation refers to the incorporation of someone hailing from another culture into a new dominant one for the purpose of them becoming a functioning member of society. This can sometimes mean that their past culture is vilified and shamed, potentially lowering this person's self-esteem and confusing their social identity. Additionally, this could also offer another explanation as to why immigrants make such easy targets for discrimination. They may not become structurally assimilated after learning the behaviour patterns of the dominant culture due to controversial disparities with their initial culture that they may regard as important.

Elaborating on what was formally touched on, what we learn in childhood shapes us by providing us with our first understandings of norms and values which we grow up with so are tough to break away from. So what happens to people who are not socialised properly? To take an extreme example, we need to look no further than the case of Genie Wiley (1957), a feral child who was neglected and abused by her family and discovered and taken into custody at the age of thirteen. Tragically, Wiley had great difficulty understanding many forms of communication as she was taught virtually nothing by the time she was found. She also struggled to learn the language whilst being rehabilitated, although some argue that this was a consequence of researchers prioritising research over Wiley's welfare.

Immorally, Western socialisation teaches an intolerance to difference within a culture. Looking back to assimilation, individuals struggling to learn the dominant culture are often blamed for their own deficiencies. This is called 'cultural deficit theory'. Those who believe it completely ignores any cultural barriers within society that prevent structural assimilation (a complete transition to the dominant culture). For example, a French-speaking immigrant struggling to learn English may be labelled as lazy or stupid and not have the lack of supportive language learning education accessible to them considered. Shockingly, this divisive theory is encouraged by capitalist societies as it removes excuses to not conform to the dominant culture that supposedly benefits all. For example, if a student influent in English undertook an IQ test for English-speaking pupils, then they might do badly on the test do inaccurate question conception and would receive grade predictions based on their grade, irrespective of the obvious cultural barriers skewing the test result.

Social Control

To maintain social order, society requires regulators that implement codes of conduct and consequents for breaking them, known as social control. The mechanisms in society imploring the acceptance of conformity and approved methods of behaviour are the social controllers. For example, the police arrest those who break the law, which is two complimentary socially controlling figures found in society. Moreover, the church may also encourage approved behaviours and attitudes based on their morality in a clericalist state.

Unfortunately, quantities of social control are not estranged to being abused by the tyrannical powers that be. We all know that in some states in the US, abortion is still illegal. Whether this is morally right or wrong is irrelevant, the point is that the social order here highly restricts personal choice in an ironically self-proclaimed liberal nation. Additionally, this regulation is usually not malleable to cater to women who have become pregnant because of rape and legally forces them into a life they did not choose. A rebellion against this is naturally caused by a desperation to take control of one's own life, which is confusingly an apparent American value in personal freedom. Controversially, this decision is highly condemned in the respective states and considered a form of murder, increasingly shaming those who wish to take control of their own destiny.

On the other hand, if there is too little social control in society, then civilian's moral compass may point in the direction of self-service, disregarding social value, therefore, empathy. For example, without the church, people may not learn to love their neighbour, nor will they care about the repercussions of their actions without a criminal justice system. To agree with the functionalist, a lack of leadership and social direction will probably ensue a selfish and violent society, but then again, too much social control limits personal freedom, so for the sake of public welfare, a balance must be found.

Social Disorder

Earlier in the chapter, it was rhetorically asked whether society was truly functional considering the existence of the chaos permeating society, including disorderly constructs such as crime and political conflict. Alas, capitalist societies indeed benefit from social divisions and inequalities as they enable conflict, which can be marketed to stimulate economic growth. Furthermore, the crime most certainly serves a purpose as it sets an example to the rest of society, unifying it in disgust and forging shared values and norms. The collateral damage of conflict leading to further crime might be considered a minor looping problem compared to the overall systematic product. The devout functionalist not only accepts social disorder; it endorses it for the establishment of power and individualistic gain through the oppression of the oppressed and the dominance of the dominant. So, society is functional, just not in the way we are sold.

Emile Durkheim

A French sociologist named Emile Durkheim lived through the industrial revolution and, like many other sociological thinkers of that time, noticed the social changes surrounding him and questioned them. The economy began to thrive, vocational opportunities were numerous, and the education system opened, so on paper, society seemed to have made equitable progress. However, Durkheim observantly recorded that as industrialisation realised the capitalist agenda over time, suicide rates were correspondingly increasing in his home country.

Contemplating the tragedies spawned via such a sinister society, the intellectual Frenchman evaluated their possible agencies. Accordingly, Durkheim identified five primary causes of immense societal discontent during the industrial revolution: individualism, excessive hope, excessive liberty, atheism, and the disvaluing of the family.

Similarly to Marx and Weber, Durkheim professed that capitalism promoted individual importance and selfishness, especially in combination with excessive hope, by enabling the grounds in which theoretically anyone can make a fortune because of the progression toward equal opportunity irrespective of bloodline nobility. Elucidatory speaking, as success is obtainable by seemingly anyone utilising enough dedication and skill, colossal pressure is burdened upon individuals to obtain wealth as if they do not, they have no excuses and will be labelled as failures by not only society but themselves too resultant of the shaming ideology infused within the socio-socioeconomic theory (harmony to Durkheim) that is capitalism.

Accelerated by rapid technological revelations, the age of enlightenment caused a decline in the perceived plausibility of religious practice. Thus Western citizens lost faith in transcendent moral values and incentives. Therefore, Western culture has been poisoned with an absolutist rejection of the afterlife determined by a person's perception of objective morality. Thus the importance of communal compassion mixed with deontological thinking was weakened into a callous culture that lacks emotional fortitude. Ironically, as any functionalist will tell us, capitalism depends on communities and shared values to function, but this sense of community is tarnished in a society absent of an ethical foundation for values to be devoutly cared about.

Consequent Mental Health Issues

Whether it be via bigotry, vilification, ridicule, devaluation, manipulation, or tyranny, the collateral damages that social order causes, as described by the functionalists themselves, have major psychological consequences. Social order gleefully endorses social division as an unwritten rule inscribed into its foundations; social isolation is the respective outcome of such divisive processes. Naturally, if traits stemming from undesirable, unpopular groups are displayed, then those who are characterised by them are shunned so intensely that their motivation to do anything productive diminishes. So, obviously, relative mental health issues like anxiety and depression will surge.

Political processes are bought, not chosen; our democratic society is absent of democracy. Following the fall of kings, we were given new ones in the form of bosses that rule us and our livelihood. Obviously, these contradictory happenings lead to mass confusion hence conflict and further social division and isolation. People simply do not know how to reach success in a society that claims it is obtainable for all; if they complain about such injustices, then they are shamed for their apparent failures by those who have obtained wealth who are so often in denial of their own lucky privileges and praise the oppressive society. Durkheim noted that this, along with many other factors like lack of government direction and transcendent incentive to endure, lead to mass selfishness and deprivation of opportunity for others, especially given the competitive nature of capitalism. Therefore, employees in Western societies have their self-esteem, self-image, developmental drive, and mental stability severely damaged by the actions and mere existence of their few decorated employers. As priorly alluded to, a tragic result of this social isolation is suicide, suicide that is unsurprisingly much less common in those with wealth than without.

If a low-wage employee who only has their labour of value is no longer motivated to work due to their oppressive societal conditions, then they may no longer have anything left to lose. Marx suggests history dictates this would result in a social uprising. The oppressed would overthrow their oppressors, and communism would destroy the processed stratification of society into socioeconomic groups, hence transitioning individualist shared values into collectivist versions. However, unlike feudalism and slavery, social classes are not assigned anymore, so perhaps the opportunity is ripe for all, and no social uprising can take place in a society where nobody truly has any options left. Nevertheless, considerations of individualism are all still relevant today as we live in an inherently individualistic society. Whichever political party leads, politicians are 'identity politics' technicians who manipulate social groups to boost their own popularity, which they will use to their own accord. For example, self-proclaimed democratic socialist Jeremy Corbyn, formally of the UK's labour party, had his disastrous 2019 political campaign criticised by popularised members of his own party for his extensive abuse of identity politics. Additionally, outside the West, in countries like Venezuela, common household items like toilet paper are not obtainable and socialist states have evidently failed to meet the basic needs of their citizenry. For without toilet paper, individual dignity, therefore, self-image cannot exactly be high. In fact, socialism's alleged impracticality is often used by capitalists to explain why socialist nations worldwide are always so socially regressive. In theory, socialism may be an antidote to the selfish, shaming nature of a capitalist society that hinders the emotional welfare of its people, but questions must be raised about the quality of life socialism produces.

Communism has proven catastrophic. Therefore it would be asinine to suggest it is a worthy contemporary when it is evidently so underdeveloped, but there are idealistically progressive ideals at its core that should be considered for the benefit of human psychological welfare in the West. This begs the question: what is more important to your mental wellbeing, individual freedom, or societal compassion?

Chapter Twelve: Social Divisions

Social Diversity

Society diversity is often described as the range of groups of people in a community. However, Dania Santana, an author and expert on multiculturalism, defines social diversity as a successful community that includes individuals from diverse groups that are all enabled to contribute to the success of the community. This means that simply having people from a variety of backgrounds is not enough to achieve social diversity. These people must be equipped with equitable rights to achieve what everybody else can. So, if a representation of these groups in the highest levels of society cannot be observed, then social diversity cannot be recognised.

For the West to boast an inclusive degree of social diversity, most of their countries will have to destroy the demand characteristics that dictate how a member of particular social groups act, in accordance with social norms that keep people in their 'places'. For instance, a black teenager living in South-East London might be stereotyped as a thug, thus, this normalised stereotype becomes a demand characteristic to subconsciously live up to via socialisation, as society functions to socialise people to conform to their shared norms and values. Consequently, demand characteristics can create self-fulfilling prophecies whereby people are pushed into disorderly social roles, like being 'forced' into crime; therefore, people in certain social groups, who have a low quality of life, usually find themselves in bad positions as they have been abandoned by their exclusive social order.

In the fight for social diversity, some politicians and television personalities commit a preference falsification. By voicing support to marginalised groups for social approval without actually having to take the progressive action required to implement change, these idols can craftily cement their socio-economic dominance. For example, many celebrities identify as democratic socialists, yet they refuse to redistribute their own massive wealth. Simply put, many idols simply do not practice what they preach.

On the other hand, an intense focus on the fight for diversity can poison the mind into developing a deluded sense of moral superiority, misinterpreting the intentions of others, and becoming too easily offended. Unfortunately, as a result of this fragile, antisocial mentality, certain prominent subcultures are influencing the behaviour of millions of people, stimulating a culture of counterintuitively exclusive behaviour in social justices warriors fighting for inclusivity. For example, today, one can be arrested for expressing acceptance of the scientific fact that biological factors between the sexes generally result in differences between male behaviour and female behaviour, such as the fact that, unlike women, men produce testosterone and are usually more aggressive and have higher sex drives. This is difficult for radical feminists to accept as they claim that differences between sexes are exclusively socially influenced, thus, they are not biologically influenced at all. As a result of their collective outrage, they accuse the rational thinkers of sexism and biological determinism; they attempt to justify their baseless accusations as the rational comments have made them feel less than when in reality, they are refused to accept the nature of their own sex out of sheer insecurity. In the end, this only spits in the face of diversity by refusing to acknowledge or 'allow for' a diverse range of beliefs in society.

Finally, in order to achieve social diversity in a uniform society, one must use chaos to implement social change. Sadly, orderly protests achieve nothing; it is only when authority is directly challenged that they might change their measures of social control. Just think, if the BLM protests in the summer of 2020 were peaceful, would they still have had inspired a societal revolt that saw enormous groups of people fight against institutional racism? No, they would not. However, this is not to say that chaotic protests are better than orderly protests. Chaos is often dangerously harmful, as is evidenced by the vandalism and disregard for social distancing seen at the BLM protests (see *Chapter Thirteen*), and when something is so undisguisable harmful, it creates a social divide. To explain, people who wished not to attend the protests saw two things: that they were automatically assumed to be racist and that the protesters were aggressive. Therefore, they grew resentful of the protesters, who already resented them; thus, some even became racist (oh good, another self-fulfilling prophecy). So, despite their somewhat 'good' intentions, protest always result in more social regression than progression.

The 'Wannabe' Oppressed: Race, Gender, and Sexual Orientation

In order to give Europe the tools that the ECHR failed to provide in order to see social groups represented diversely, many countries activated legislation that focused on how to equitably reduce the social barriers that some social groups face in life. For example, the UK protected nine social groups from discrimination with both the Queen's and parliament's commencement of the Equality Act 2010. However, despite recognising that different members of different social groups are often met with discriminatory abuse, the UK still failed to completely alter the behaviours of racists, homophobes, and sexists for the better, albeit in ways that might not be so obvious to begin with. See, people of many different cultural backgrounds live in the West. Therefore, direct acts of homophobia and sexism that are truly oppressive are rarely seen, especially given the law, cancel culture, and an oh-so Western social etiquette that perpetuates oversensitivity. However, that is not to say that these forms of discrimination never happen. For instance, casual yet indirect racism is incredibly common and can be found in everyday comments such as "oh no Tyrone, there is absolutely nothing wrong with sounding black". Here, despite the good intention, the accreditation of an urban trait to a group makes social disregard apparent, even if it is unconscious. Although, it is so important to note that there is a difference between ignorance and malicious racism; just because someone said something racist does not mean that they are racist. Rather, it could just mean that they are ignorant. Mind and behaviour are different.

Similar to how some fat people say that not wanting to be fat, for whatever reason, is fatphobic, critical race theorists accuse people of being racist due to their unavoidable whiteness, meaning that anyone who is not black or is content with not being black, is in fact racist. This 'pipeline' mindset demotivates people to stop trying to act inclusively and radicalises them into prejudice as, according to the accusers, that is what they are and there is nothing that can do to change that.

It is also difficult to see racism against black ppl as it is shut down quickly; against white people, it is not so. On Twitter, for example, white people are commonly overgeneralised in a negatively stereotypical and slanderous fashion. Amusingly, this discrimination is typically justified through reference to slavery. Revenge. Revenge against people not involved in something that happened over 100 years ago but seen fit for abuse due to sharing a colour of skin. Clearly, these idiots need to be made aware that the white people of today are not the same people as the slave owners. They are just a part of the same socially constructed ethnic group in an utterly different world. If white people are all still racist, are black people all still slaves?

Moreover, the LGBT community has been heavily ridiculed for its ridiculous outrage in response to mundane and trivially inoffensive affairs. Say, according to the eternally intellectual trans-rights advocate, should a person dare to assume the gender of an individual with bushy chest hair, a long beard, and a nine-inch penis, they must surely be transphobic. In the most attention-seeking fashion, this sort of radical leftist ideology diminishes attention from people who are actually experiencing oppression and ensures that the public stop taking the LGBT(Q+... "ugh") community as a holistic entity seriously due to their members' illogical reasoning.

It is this very tendency of the exaggeration of the suffrage of the LGBT community that people are critical of pride month, not because they are homophobic, but because pride is unnecessary. To put it plainly, Westerners almost entirely feel indifferent towards homosexuality and accept homosexual behaviour as morally sound, yet they are constantly told that they individually contribute to a society that marginalises gay, lesbian, bisexual, and transgender people, which removes any creditability to the complaints of the community (with an ironically intense volume of infighting). Thus, should a situation arise whereby the rights of the LGBT community are restricted, aside from their own inventions, then those complaining will be seen much like 'the gay who cried wolf'.

In regards to sexism, no one can deny that gender norms have historically been socialised into people throughout their lives to functionally place women into lesser social positions than men. Specifically, one must only look back to the twentieth century where little girls were taught to prepare for the role of a housewife for their future husbands. Today though, equality is aggressively maintained through legislation, welfare states, and social upheaval; the glass ceiling stands as a myth spread by wealthy liberal feminists who are really just chasing a larger pay package. Take female footballers, for example, Hope Solo and Alex Morgan, two players for the USA women's team, who have accused FIFA of institutional sexism as male footballers are paid much more than they are. However, the soccer sensations fail to recognise why. Hopefully, the following points might help to clear their confusion:

    1. Men are much better at football than women.
        a. See Dallas u21s 5-2 USA Women.
    2. Men's football makes more money than women's football, so there is obviously going to be more money in it.
    3. Men are much, much better at football than women.
        a. See Australia Women 0-7 Newcastle Jets u15s.

It is also worth mentioning that gender roles play an active role in the mental health between the sexes, although it might not be what the more radical feminists expect. As boys are socialised into being masculine, they are less likely to open up about their feelings. Comparable to how the wartime British slogan 'keep calm and carry on' still urges people to push through strife and stop complaining about how unfair and needless it is for them, gender roles have stigmatised men who struggle emotionally as feeble cowards for not 'manning up', an impeccable example of what toxic masculinity truly means. Subsequently, as they cannot talk to anyone about their feelings, men must learn to live with them, although in the process, they become a ticking timebomb ready to explode in a fit of suppressed depression., this is why the biggest killer of men under fifty is suicide. Depressed men kill themselves as their voices are smothered by a toxic sea of stigma. If one were to take the abortionist argument and apply it here, they should say that women know nothing of the male struggle. Therefore they cannot comment for their lack of experience leads them incapable of empathy. Fair? Do not think too hard.

To supplement the idea that women might actually be treated better than men in the West, one must only look to the nature of divorces. Statistically, a divorced mother will almost always retain child custody over the father, irrespective of their suitability. If society was truly weighed in favour of men, then they would not be so repeatedly deprived of fatherhood.

The Oppressed: Religion

There are many people in the UK who identify as religious, who all possess the ability to vote, invest, drive and do what everybody else does (see the Equality Act 2010). According to a 2018 survey from *Eurostats*, 59.8% of the UK's population are religious, meaning that there is an extensive collection of religious people who are comfortable enough to be outspoken about their beliefs. Additionally, there is a noticeably diverse range of religions practised in the UK, albeit with Christianity remaining the primary faith, accounting for 52.6% of the population.

Within Western society, religious influence is impossible to ignore. As Jordan Peterson states in his book '12 Rules for Life's, the Judaeo-Christian worldview dogmatises people in their primary and secondary socialisation. Consequently, we are morphed into conformity with Western culture's collective values, norms, and even legislation based upon religious code of ethics. Therefore, it is undeniable that a strong social diversity amongst religious people is represented in the West, with the fortification of their rights through borderline clericalism. However, when the ONS studied the proportion of people working in a high-skilled occupation by religion across England and Wales in 2018, they discovered that these roles were disproportionately more likely to be awarded to those of the Christian faith, who are 28% likely to be working in a high-skilled occupation, as opposed to Muslims, who were only 21.3% likely. From the same study, this becomes especially concerning when looking at the fact that Muslims (34.5%) are more likely to complete degree-level education than Christians (30%). Therefore, outlining a lack of opportunity (thus diversity) for Muslims as they are typically more highly educated than Christians yet are deprived of the opportunity to grow their careers to merely the same level.

Despite its apparent lack of interreligious diversity at present, Western countries, like England, are becoming increasingly religiously diverse. The UK government has revealed plans to boost the security for 49 places of worship across various religions. Highlighting the perceived importance of religious diversity from the perspective of the British government, but of course, this extra security would not be required without the existence of consistent hate crime and vandalising towards religious people and landmarks.

Outside the West, in radically Islamic countries like Iran and Afghanistan, the law is based on Sharia. In these countries, the worship of false idols is punishable by death. Hence, according to Dawn (2014), there is a low level of religious social diversity. This is because the teachings of the Quran are taken so far that an intolerance of other religions is enforced. This is unlike more religiously social diverse Western countries, like the UK and Australia, where hate speech is outlawed to protect certain social groups, say by the UK's Public Order Act

1986. This means that, as a social group, religious people are heavily protected by Western governments.

Still, what is the public opinion on religion? Well, Richard Dawkins, the popular English author of the widely criticised book 'The God Delusion', claims that ridicule is a more favourable debate method to religious people rather than serious objective argument, stating that not engage Religious people in serious debate". Obviously, this is a cowardly, socially regressive, and ignorant take on social etiquette that sees sound objective arguments ignored and the spread of information is intercepted between cultures, destroying the functions of education as one knows it, in the most ironically primitive of fashions. Additionally, due to Dawkins' popularity, it is evidence of an intense irreligious sentiment that impedes the rights of religious people as a consequence of the Equality Act 2010. If one has good arguments, then they should be encouraged to voice them for the benefit of others; academic theologians have historically had reasonable arguments against the irreligious worldview, such as William Lane Craig, a contemporary philosopher who popularised the Kalam cosmological argument, who proclaims that science itself is a philosophy. Should one resort to ridicule, however, they indirectly indicate that people like Dawkins do not have any objective arguments, strengthening the man of faith's argument validity. Specifically, this is an atheist ignorance demonstrating that the person who discouraged interpersonal communication and debate actually lacks the capacity to make an informed decision on their position on religion or cosmology. Yet, the same people will characterise religious people based on stigmatised views about their supposedly 'blind' faith. Since so many people not just endorse but literally just celebrate this level of narrow-minded discrimination, then that it proves that Britain does not need increased levels of education regarding religious inclusion, but instead rehabilitation of new-atheists.

Western regions are permeated with philosophical absolutists. Religious zealots, to provide an avid example, are mocked for their irrational views on scientific theories like evolution as they disregard any quantitative data. A fair reaction. Though, what if a person neglects all qualitative data. For example, a football pundit could never draw opinions solely from stats (quantitative data) without watching games (qualitative data). Not only would they convey terribly invalid opinions as a result, but they would also be ridiculed by the masses. Yet, people like Dawkins, who disregard all qualitative data regarding cosmology, are admired as intellectual thinkers. These social norms and shared values are proof of a societal bias against faith and the credibility of qualitative thinking in the West.

Many self-proclaimed rationalists also love Jordan Peterson's work until they stumble across his prominent use of religious stories, then they contort their view on his work in light of his belonging to a particular social group. This spits in the face of objective critical analysis; to have your supposedly critical evaluation of a text that you found intellectually stimulating forcibly changed when learning of the author's social characteristics is to have your judgement clouded by bias. 'Critics' who administer this embarrassingly poor display of cognitive malfunction represent a stellar example of what is wrong with Western society. People are characterised by their assignment to social constructed social groups. Peterson, for example, had readers accept his ideas are rational by reactionary imbeciles before they unearthed the horrifying existence of his personal religious beliefs, which caused these culturally conditioned inbreeds (tribalism) to instantly renounce any support of his work. This, in the UK, must be considered literal discrimination. To devalue a person's beliefs purely on the basis of their religious beliefs is to violate the Equality Act 2010, which lists religion as a protected characteristic, much like sexual orientation, race, gender, and disability. This also highlights how unopen the West is to new ideas; if a catholic came over to your house to tell you that it is on fire, would you disbelieve them as they are catholic? You are a fool if you would consider the social characteristics of a person before their words and actions; you cannot play monopoly with the truth as to do so is to commit (yet another, well done!) logical fallacy via 'label and dismiss'.

Westerners must read widely because before one can hold an informed opinion, they must be fully informed. Wisdom is wisdom; the source is irrelevant.

The Oppressed: Disability

In the UK, Government attempts equity for the disabled via legislation like the Equality Act 2010, which defines "disability" as a protected characteristic, outlawing "discrimination arising from disability" and implements a "duty to make adjustments" so disabled people have sufficient access to the same services non-disabled people do. As reported by the BBC, in 2018, a paraplegic service user sued London airport for failing to comply with this legislation, thus depriving them of a service they paid for due to the service provider's neglect to provide him with a wheelchair. Societal attitudes like this strengthen the notion that disabled people's rights are commonly overlooked in Western culture, despite the support for equality from the national government. Interestingly, this is the opposite of the social diversity problem for religious Westerners.

That said, some countries have passed laws supporting caregivers to provide the necessary care for disabled people, demonstrating an equitable solution to meet the needs of disabled people. Additionally, first-world countries like the UK have outlawed deprivation of liberty, meaning that even if a caregiver believes their client is making a dangerous decision, they are prohibited from enforcing restrictions on them for the perceived benefit of their safety and should instead try to persuade the disabled person to make a more informed decision (Care Act 2014). Also, should they possess the capacity to make independent decisions (otherwise, caregivers should act in their best interest, as enforced by the Mental Capacity Act 2005), the disabled person's personal choice is final, and their preferences should be attempted to be met. This champions a person-centred approach to disabled people's care and encourages personal choice and freedom.

Recently, inspiring social messages of empowerment like 'enabled not disabled' have helped reduce the stigma around disabled people today. This message was popularised by Ryan Raghoo, an Olympic long jumper who competed in the 2016 Paralympics. The Paralympics themselves have also proven to be an effective and celebrated method of representation. Not only does it allow access to competitive sport for disabled people, but the event is also watched worldwide and taken very seriously, with the participants sincerely admired for their technical proficiencies, not their disabilities.

Tragically though, consistently negative representation in film has added to stigma permeating disability by characterising disabled people by their conditions and inadvertently suggesting that people with physical disabilities are resentful of others and grow a tendency to commit crimes. Moreover, as discovered by a team of scholars when studying the rates of bullying in schools internationally, "children with disabilities were two to three times more likely to be bullied than their non-disabled peers". This can explain the ONS's 2019 research that indicates disabled people are less likely to obtain any qualification when compared to their non-disabled peers because they would be more likely to drop out to avoid facing bullies or lose their incentive to study as the discrimination they endure might play on their mind.

Disabled people are also less likely than non-disabled people to be employed. According to the UK government, in 2020, "51.4 per cent of disabled people are in employment - 28.1 percentage points lower than for non-disabled people". Other than incapacity, one explanation for this could be the failure of disabled people to obtain any qualifications, meaning that the discrimination of disabled people in early life has led to further inequality later.

'TikTok', a Chinese video-sharing social media platform, has exploded in Western popularity since emerging from the tainted ashes of the paedophile-riddled atrocity 'Musical.ly' and provides a stark example of the First World's thoroughly second-class values.

On TikTok, social groups (minority or not) are collectively under consistent abuse and marginalisation. For example, physically disabled people have their comments filled with ridicule for physical features out of their control, as if some people did not face enough issues in a society seemingly allergic to equity. Again, this repulsive behaviour does not exactly do wonders for anyone's self-esteem or quality of life.

Tragically, conformity is the culture of the day, and TikTok perpetuates it. See, the more discriminatory content goes viral, the more that content is encouraged to be produced as everyone wants to go viral. Unfortunately, TikTok either has not quite figured this out, or more likely they want to ignore it entirely as it drags more idiots over to their fittingly idiotic app. Not only does TikTok have an antisocial behaviour problem, but it also causes antisocial behaviour. Come to think of it, it causes that in more ways than one (looking at you, overstimulation).

Fundamentally, TikTok is centred on shock-value, actively encouraging and promoting content depicting 'savage' discriminatory humour and underage sexual objectification. This is perhaps why TikTok refuses to amend their insipid community guidelines that strategically allow for users to post sexually explicit content through their menially vague rules that they systematically fail to carry out or properly regulate (see *Chapter Six*).

Additionally, in 2019, following a damning research report by a German digital rights group, TikTok reluctantly admitted to suppressing the videos made by users who were either "ugly", "abnormal", "too wrinkly", "living in slums", and more, in an 'effort' the prevent bullying. Well, one can only really say well done to TikTok there. What a great job they did in depriving certain people of a platform to 'protect' them, so congratulations...

Clearly, it is important to underline that TikTok, much like any other social media platform, enforces cruel and unobtainable body images. A typical verified user, to illustrate, is the generalised personification of what is deemed physically attractive across the West, especially since TikTok depends on Western advertisement and usage to maintain its success. Consequently, many service users will have their self-images derailed, thus depleting their self-esteem and then their general happiness. Notably, this is also a common cause of great depression and anxiety, which can also lead to suicide, something that is particularly common in female teens. One cannot begin to imagine why...

Conceivably, at least to the disillusioned few, disabled people are far, far more oppressed than black people, gay people, or God forbid, women. Whilst society's shared values are more ambiguous when it comes to religion, the characteristics of gender, race, and sexual orientation remain fully protected, both legislatively and socially speaking. In fact, in light of the (over)protection of these characteristics, especially when involving interpersonal communication, it is disgustingly astounding one what can get away with when speaking to an autistic person or a Christian.

Tribalism: A Recipe for Social Exclusion

Literally, the term 'tribalism' refers to a societal state whereby people are organised into tribes: social divisions linked by blood, culture, and a recognised leader. Contemporary social critics frequently describe Western society as being tribalistic due to how attitudes stemming from a religious loyalty to one's own social group invoke a type of tribalistic ignorance towards other cultural behaviours and beliefs. For example, there is an ethnic tribalism plaguing Western civilisation with a conceptual tribal warfare pitting white and black people against each other (see *Chapter Six*), upheld by the pseudo-activism of extremists. Consequently, such an "us vs them" mentality only accomplishes further segregation via a perpetuation of social polarisation.

If the tribalistic nature of Western societies has achieved anything, it is to underline the hypocritical bigotry of the regressive left by spotlighting their precious "us vs them" mentality. Clearly, left-wing tribalists are aware of the differences between individuals in their own groups but not of others (willingly or not). Thus, they wilfully characterise members of other tribes as identically uniform, perhaps suggesting that negative stereotypes should not be applied to gay people whilst viewing all religious people are zealous homophobes, irrespective of their personal interpretations of scripture. It is simply impossible to take them seriously.

Capitalism teaches individual accountability. Therefore, there is always a target for blame, other than the government, especially in times of economic crisis. So, inside this inescapably individualistic West, individuals within social groups are often scapegoated out of frustration as the sole reason a social group does not achieve their shared goals (highly contrary to the 'team' mentality of the 'tribes'), with ignorance of their ideological malfunctions. To be scapegoated is to be targeted, pressurised, and kicked from the tribe, so to speak; to be labelled as the sole cause for blame and uproar. It does nobody any service, yet it is so imperative to the survival of the grotesque conformity that sees that the most popular, hyperbolic beliefs also equate to the most validated. The person scapegoated knows that they have been treated unfairly. The same is also true for social groups, but at least they share the pressure.

'Cultural appropriation' is another phrase that has recently become a part of every liberal arts student's lexicon. It infers that the importance of shared values trump that of individual values and that conformed behaviour within fundamentally unified social groups is mandatory. People who believe this are idiots, idiots who ironically could form the criteria for another selective social group of their own. Then they could claim every other idiot is appropriating their culture.

If it has its menacing way, the overarching Western culture pierces the citizen's brain and rips away their capacity for compassionate cognition, instead masking it with an inauthentic substitute concerned with an apathetic empathy for others, activating only when one is instinctively alerted to the opportunity of caressing their tribes perception of their virtue, typically through the violent murder of a rival tribesman's reputation which, once lost, is unregainable. Truly, it is with great sadism that modern men desolate the lives of others and strive to quench their own insatiable, vampiric bloodlust.

So, if the West is stuck in this divisive cycle of tribalism, how can it socially progress into something better? According to Dostoevsky, social progression is an endless striving progress that dooms humans to feel nothing but anguish; new problems will forever replace those that are eliminated by social change to guarantee societal discontent and strife. Thus, regardless of a tribe's ideas for social progression, they all stand as futile in the end.

Albert Camus once said, "man is the only creature that refuses to be what he is."

So remember kids, conformity is cancer.

Chapter Thirteen: Criminal Justice

Western Criminal Justice Systems

Western criminal justice systems (CJSs) use various methods and volumes of social control to minimise the effects and rates of crime across their respective societies. In particular, the UK's investigative practices depend on the strict use of quantitative data drawn from the 'Office of National Statistics' (ONS) and industry records to make generalisable but somewhat invalid assumptions about who might be most likely of committing a crime in order to narrow down suspects before questioning them. In contrast, the US's investigative practices hinge on more qualitative data in the form of detectives' educated opinions based on a great depth of information that is vulnerable to interpretation biases. Resultantly, different CJSs vary in methodological reliability and validity, therefore, they each have their own strengths and weaknesses in attempting to respond to criminal offences, catch offenders, protect victims, reduce crimes, and so on.

When compared to the rest of the world, Western CJSs offer more humanistic treatment to offenders. Generally speaking, European prisons provide more rehabilitation services and better living conditions for prisoners than in, say, South American prisons, whereby systematically corrupted prisons employ guards that can be bribed for illegal entry for drug dealing purposes. However, despite the flickering glimmer of sympathy for the benefits of processes such as rehabilitation, the West's use of it staggers across its sovereign states. In the UK, for example, high crime rates and crowded prisons mean that there is little room for rehab, unlike the so-called socialist country of Norway, where higher taxes are used to redistribute money to the welfare state that funds 'better' prisons. Although, the reality is substantially more complex than this.

Similar to other Scandinavian prisons, and even institutions in other European countries like Germany, Norwegian prisons are renowned for their effective rehab programs, usually completely reforming offenders, and the provision of lenient prisoner freedom and quality of life, ensuring that prisoners feel comfortable in their rooms (not 'cells') equipped with televisions and video game consoles. Conversely, UK prisons have been heavily criticised for their dehumanisation of prisoners and refusal to rehabilitate them, something that is commonly attributed to the high degree of repeat offending. However, in Wales, an emulation of the Norwegian prison system was unsuccessfully attempted. A diluted order only served chaos as prisoners took advantage of guards who had their sense of hierarchal superiority destroyed in favour of loosening the obvious power imbalance to fight prisoner isolation. Conceivably, the UK cannot introduce more humanistic prisons as of yet for crime rates are too high, yet they also cannot theoretically reduce crime rates without the use of rehabilitation services. Though, perhaps with great effort, innovation, and societal unification, enough social transformation could be caused to force the shared norms and values of British society to change in a way that naturally reduces crime rates. These shared values would, eventually, be represented in prison life, like in

Scandinavia. Therefore, instead of crime being labelled as a social disorder by a structural-functionalist society, the UK's newly socialist method of thinking could stimulate enough progressive change in society that lowers crimes rates, which lowers prison population, which founds opportunity for rehabilitation, which reduces the chances of repeat offences, which further lowers crime rates, thus making us more like Norway, rather than a country that has to endlessly produce more and more prisons to house ever-growing criminals in a society that only gives them one option.

Given, this is a left-wing idea, but this does not mean that an inherently left-wing society is at all practical. With a CJS focussed on the rehabilitation of offenders, rather than their harsh punishment as a measure of light social control, a society coupled with an incentivising free-market will encourage people to be their very best selves that, should the government fail to balance the need for tediously 'left' and 'right-wing' ideals, they would otherwise not. Conclusively, it is only by the eye of a disillusioned radical centrist that a society could be fair, just, and most prominently, functioning.

Evaluations of Contemporary Criminal Justice

People tend to have conflicting opinions on certain CJSs, depending on their political affiliations. In the UK, the left-wing labour party condemns the CJS as the punishment of offenders is ineffective because offenders are labelled as deviant and labelling theories can become self-fulfilling prophecies, causing repeat offending. Also, they voice concern about the lack of rehabilitation, which they support through the endorsement of social learning theory, a behaviourist theory suggesting that people learn new attitudes and behaviours from other people in their immediate environment. Thirdly, labour claims that the shared norms of this largely conservative nation are oppressive and restrict people from being their ideal selves. Instead, they are cursed to live as their true self, a self that has not realised their ambitions via physical experience. OK, perhaps the latter point would be a bit too philosophical for the labour party, but existentialists would agree with that specific left-wing sentiment.

Opposing the UK's more left-wing, prominent party are the conservative who are, astoundingly(!), right-wing, or at least always more right-wing than labour. As the UK is already a sovereign state with a capitalistic socio-economic societal base, conservatives typically do not wish to invoke much social change in society, hence, also within the CJS. Instead, conservatives will criticise labour views as utopian and as their solutions unrealistic, simply because crime cannot be abolished. The only way of combatting crime is to intensify measures of social control, such as with the introduction of harsher sentencing and omniscient surveillance, so as to reduce the potential reward of criminal behaviour whilst increasing the risk associated with it, too, thus scaring off potential offenders. To justify such restrictions of liberty, conservatives argue that breaking the law is to endanger society as the law embodies the functional shared values of society that exist for the benefit of British people. Naturally, such a claim is heavily disputed, even within this very text.

French socialist Michel Foucault expressed great hatred for France's twentieth-century CJS. Comparing it to medieval CJSs, he said that prison today looks kinder than it really is as simply killing offenders is far less common, however, ancient CJSs were so obviously cruel that they inspired social rebellions, whereas the modern CJS deceitfully disguises its cruelty by taking away long periods of life that 'teach' and 'punish' offenders, practically killing them anyway. Foucault's unique criticism of modern criminal justice can remind people that there are many different forms of evil and that

Western civilisation may not be as developed or progressive as one may assume.

Another common accusation from the 'left' is that prosecutors are corrupt and rely on false evidence to incriminate people that they deem threatening to their power. However, drawing a guilty verdict on the basis of a DNA test result, for instance, is often considered a prosecutor fallacy by the 'right', who claim that the potential for quantitative data to be biased by human error, be wrong, or be intentional manipulated overrules the principles of true justice. This highlights how baseless accusations and assumptions are thrown in the direction of the other tribe, figuratively speaking, in order to make them look bad in the public eye, regardless of what the truth may be.

More Political Biases and Victimhood

Liberal-minded individuals in the West have often accused the CJS of institutional racism. For example, more racial profiling seems to occur in poorer areas, as a trademark policing practice, such as in the poverty-stricken South London. However, this is simply due to the UK CJS's quantitative approach to catching offenders in South London, an area largely populated by ethnic minorities. Of course, these critics can also claim that ethnic minorities should be given equal opportunities so as to not be housed in poorer areas, but legislative changes (Equality Act 2010; Human Rights Act 1998) can serve to protect the rights and combine systems of equality and equity to stimulate a gradual growth of social diversity across the country, thus counteracting this perceived problem. Granted, this is a work in progress, but social progression is never instant.

On the other hand, some of the alt-right have claimed that individuals from foreign countries receive lighter sentencing than native people in Western countries. In the

UK, for instance, a Muslim immigrant killed policeman Lee Rigby but pleaded insanity and was admitted into a psychiatric ward in Broadmoor with little media coverage of the incident. Critics have asked, "what if the killer was white" and "is illness applied consistently across the races?". Although, some of the alt-left ask the same questions with the roles reversed. They claim that 'white people' in the US receive 'easier' sentencing in psychiatric facilities, unlike ethnic minorities who are seemingly rarely granted such as supposed privilege. All things considered, Western courts actually apply their manslaughter sentencing consistently when considering appeals of insanity. Rather, it is political biases that skew reality in ways that are compliant with the interpretations of delusional tribes.

Black lives matter (BLM) protesters across the West have been both praised by the majority of the 'left' and criticised by the majority of the 'right'. Whilst the 'left' sympathises with the protesters' apparent dissatisfaction with civil rights and social inequality relating to race, the 'right' denounces protesters for vandalising both public and private property, such as historical statues and small business stores, respectively. Irrespective of this, one thing that BLM protesters must be criticised for is their collective ignorance of the interests of public health during a literal pandemic. Across the summer of 2020, massive congregations of moronic goblins would utterly ignore the scientifically-informed need to wear a mask and maintain social distancing to protect the wellbeing of citizens. Despite the high recovery rates of people who have suffered from COVID-19, millions of people have still died. Whilst in remains only a minority of people are deemed fatally vulnerable to coronavirus, one could still transmit the virus to another living with a compromised immune system or respiratory issues when they do not adherence to infection control regulations. In something of a postmodern world, people have their own truths that are usually based on what political goons they like to follow, whether they have the self-awareness to see it or not, and all of them will delude them in a time of global crisis. Across the West, there are clusters of enlightened sages all claiming that COVID-19 is a hoax, social distancing is a violation of their human rights, or that face masks are toxic as they force people to 'inhale their own carbon dioxide' (see *Chapter Ten*). Such wisdom could only be bestowed to the masses via the common Westerner, preferably through a social media post, who must also believe that people living with diabetes also live an expendable life. Thinking back to BLM protesters who wilfully sacrifice the safety of an entire nation to 'fight the bigger picture' ("what's good, Stalin?"), police were even scared to make arrests for vandals for fear of being labelled racist. Think about that for a second, people were literally too scared to do their literal job because Karen and her four-thousand art student friends from Kent would have all crawled out of their *Fiat 500*s together to baselessly accused them of institutional racism. What a poetically humanistic and rational realm the West is.

On the off chance that one may not have noticed, being oppressed is pretty trendy. In fact, "racism" is such an overused word that is has lost all meaning; being called "racist" is more a part of tribal warfare where the accuser might earn a hypothetical badge and honour... well, honour and sympathy for services to the CDE (Claims Devoid of Evidence – *citation needed*). Despite what Western society would have you ignorantly believe, racism is defined as discrimination against someone for their ethnicity, rather than a "straight-white-male-bigot" voting republican. At the risk of sounding like Alex Jones, almost all white people experience racism daily. On social media, for example, being anti-white is the fashion and one could express these views free of consequence. If a white person were to overgeneralise black people as a black person might overgeneralise white people, then they would be immediately 'cancelled' as they have passed judgement maliciously onto another solely based on the colour of their skin, something that 'woke' people would never do... Seriously though, regarding the popularity of claiming one is being oppressed without evidence, an individual actually experiencing racism is perceived to be more of a boy crying wolf, even by the left, ironically. This is because the unfounded claims of people pretending to fight for social justice contribute largely to the perpetuation of racism due to two instances of collateral damage: the divide it creates between the races, and its respective self-fulfilling prophecy (labelling theory) that will never stop its fulfilment (white people becoming racist) unless victimhood loses its status as a shared value of society.

Behaviourism and Rehabilitation

According to behaviourists, people have their behaviours taught to them in their developmental stages, through classic and operant conditioning, therefore, their behaviour can be changed by the same means of socialisation. This resocialisation of individuals is called rehabilitation, at least when a practitioner is trying to replace an undesirable behaviour in an individual with a desirable one, and is used to destroy deviant behaviours. Thus, bringing subjects into social unity, conformity. Despite its seemingly totalitarian undertones, rehabilitation is inherently humanistic and it is only truly effective when the subject is shown empathy, not characterised by their past mistakes, and given a platform to be their best self. It recognises the potential for social influences to control people's choices and assumes that people are not always responsible for their own actions, for, rehabilitation is underpinned by social learning theory.

Granted, it is true that some people can never be rehabilitated, but it cannot be known who these people are until rehabilitation is attempted. Therefore, rehabilitation must always be attempted to avoid presuming individuals as incapable of changing, such as with those living with ASPD. Individuals living with anti-social personality disorder are classified as being incapable of experiencing empathetic thought processes, however, this does not render them incapable of being productive members of society that lead good and meaningful lives. Despite their gift of nonchalance, these people are not an indistinguishable collective of callous and superficially charming opportunists; they are individuals. Therefore, should they fall into crime, they must be helped up. Otherwise, they will only fall further.

As previously expressed, the correct social conditions must be in place in society for rehabilitation to function. To elaborate, a radicalised child may become racist before they have legally had the capacity to make informed decisions and carry these views into their adult life, where they are deemed to have the capacity although they have already been socialised to believe what they do. Consequently, they are unfairly characterised by their current mindset and punished by the state. After their sentence, society's social order confirms that they will craftily continue to be punished as the characterisation of their self by others perpetuates as they are still classified as a 'racist' because of their past actions. Subsequently, they are denied any chance of redemption and are socially isolated. Such conditions may create feelings of resentment to society and this former racist may once again become racist, such are the joys and wonders of labels. Here, both left and right-wing ideals cause events so tragic that rehabilitation may not even help a person back into society. How can one conform in a society that will always hate them?

The Criminalisation of Deviance and Subsequent Mental Health Issues

Whilst there are key differences between deviant and criminal behaviour, sociologists across the political landscape, from Marxists to neoliberals, agree that Western society intends to criminalise deviance, rather than behaviour that poses a form of threat to others.

Labelling theorists suggest that negative labelling causes people to define themselves as deviant, thus they begin to act in ways that deviate from social norms. For example, a South-East London teenager living on a council estate may be stigmatised as a thug, therefore, thinking that they are in fact a 'thug', they join a gang and commit knife crimes. Additionally, this may serve to explain why upper-class people's deviant behaviour is excused. To explain, wealthy individuals are presumed to be conformists, even when they are secretly deviant, unlike working-class people who are stigmatised as criminals if they are poor and punished harsher for petty crimes.

Social constructionists claim that being labelled negatively can affect a person's life chances and mental health. For example, the negative stigma attached to socially constructed diagnoses of mental illness is a method of medicalising deviance, as a person who is depressed is deviating from normative behaviours; therefore, they are labelled accordingly, a process that further demotivates and isolates the already depressed individual. The situation is similar to criminalising deviance. Deviance behaviours, such as ridiculing the ruling monarch of the commonwealth in the commonwealth, are made punishable by law to encourage conformity to the government's wishes. When a person is labelled as a 'criminal', their life begins to crumble. They suffer from self-devaluation, a loss of personal income, a loss of relationships, a personal demoralisation, and an accelerated fear of social rejection.

Justifying the criminalisation of deviance, social control theorists suggest that deviant behaviour is inherently rational, just like human beings (aww, how humanistic), who are naturally selfish and violent creatures. Therefore, they must be controlled. Of course, such a decree of biological determinism theoretically neglects the obvious social factors that contribute to the development of deviant behaviour, so anyone holding this opinion should genuinely be embarrassed with themselves (looking at you, John Major).

The Ethics of Criminal Justice

The ethics of the CJS really come down to two things: empathy for the individual versus justice for the collective. The matter is obviously subjective, however, if judges, juries, probation officers, prosecutors, and the ridiculously tribalistic public were to actually contemplate how simply attempting to empathise with individual people could lead to a massive reform of collective offenders, thus, saving everyone from dangerous crime. Instead, Western society uses the CJS system to excessively punish offenders and bother not to nurture them back into society, evidenced by constant reoffending.

It is not the fault of the criminal that they cannot find peace from the laws of a place that pushes them so far into crime. Crime is their only option, as long as they feel that it is.

Chapter Fourteen: Healthcare

Historical and Modern Approaches to Healthcare

The legendary ancient Greek philosopher Aristotle is credited with authoring the idea of four fundamental elements: earth, fire, water, and wind. Eventually, this would form the basis of the first scientific approach to medicine with the naturalistic theory of the 'four humours'. Associated with its respective natural development climates, phlegm (deemed to be produced in the brain) was linked to water and correlated with the seasons of winter and spring due to the higher bodily production rates observed within those times. To treat an unbalanced production of phlegm, Doctors instructed 'patients' to partake in activities heavily involving hot and dry sensations as they were the antithesis of the cold and wet conditions causing excessive phlegm production. Thankfully, the primitive naturalistic medical approach was phased out in favour of the reliable biomedical approach, which of course could not exist without the theoretical foundations built by Aristotle's revolutionary revelations.

Come the early seventeenth century, French-born scientist René Descartes devised the theory of mind-body dualism which described the mind and body as two separate entities, suggestively dawning 'the age of enlightenment'. Accordingly following this pioneering notion, logical medical theories such as specific aetiology (medicine searching for specific causes of illness) and the mechanical metaphor (the human body is built of interacting functional components like a machine) to further expand a rational comprehension of medicine and medical conditions. However, the esteemed biomedical model of health truly began after the nineteenth-century principle of objective science utilising the characteristically scientific tools of quantitative data measurement, empiricism, hypothesis testing, and physical causes.

Illness and Disease

Diseases are empirically measured and physically studied; truths unravelled by objective science have undoubtedly contributed most beneficially to the saving of many, many lives. Crucially, the understanding of biochemical cause and effect relationships between diseases and their linked symptoms has unleashed the genius of scientists in developing remarkable pharmaceutical cures to help the world and formed worthy recognition of these natural magicians as the heroes they are. Despite intercultural differentiation of the qualitative interpretation of diseases like pinta, a harmless tropical disease causing skin discolouration, the objective symptomatic results of contracting diseases remain a scientific truth. Still, denunciations are hurled at the societal machines where these scientists function as but unsuspecting pawns controlled by their tyrannical masters who seek to entrap the masses into a manipulative sense of social unity. Cunningly, illness is socially constructed to fortify the shared norms of society. For example, the normative definition of health underpins a moral dimension that claims people living with obesity, sexually transmitted illnesses, or substance addictions have irresponsibly self-inflicted themselves and must be displayed as a consequential threat of deviance from cultural conformity. Irrespective of their reality, there is no empirical method of measuring illnesses therefore they can be whatever the medical world wishes; illness can perform whatever societal function a governing authority desires. For example, gender dysphoria is a socially constructed illness used to diagnose people experiencing a dissociation with their presently assigned gender, another social construct separate from biological sex. This harmful diagnosis functions to alienate transgender people from society and spread the message that something is medically wrong with a person who feels that they were tragically born in the wrong body, therefore the idea that transgenderism is unhealthy and freakish becomes societal shared norms and values.

The Objectivity of Health

As illuded to heretofore, various definitions of health exist, thus, much controversy hovers over the phenomenon ideologies of good and bad health. Health, as a state of mental and physical well-being, has an element of social construction regarding collective perceptions on the quality of health. For example, problems always arise in attempts to quantify physical health using the body mass index (BMI) valuing system as it fails to account for muscle mass and assumes an absolute normative definition of health when considering what is underweight or overweight. Furthermore, these variables are once again assessed differently depending on the social influence within a culture because obesity was once considered a sign of wealth and healthy well-being, rather than the modern take being that there will be a deficiency of exercise or an excessive eating disorder contributing to a person's obesity. Therefore, if scientists wish to empirically measure physical health, then they must willingly ignore external social and mental contributing factors to protect their biased studies. Moving on from the normative definition of health, validity issues continue to permeate objective attempts of accounting for health in the functional, negative, and optimal approaches. Firstly, the functional definition of health hinges on the assumption that societal barriers to people labelled 'disabled' is a fault of these individuals rather than the inequitable environment. Secondly, the optimal definition of health asserts that undeniable homeostasis in health exists, yet it fails to explain how this optimal balance is determined. Thirdly and finally, the negative definition (underpinning the biomedical model of health) mistakenly makes the claim that for a person to be considered scientifically healthy they must be free of illness, illness obviously being a social construct. Hence, what constitutes the quality of personal health is entirely subjective and cannot be accounted for using the scientific method.

In 1973, American psychologist David Rosenhan conducted an infamous experiment that involved the infiltration of multiple psychiatric facilities. The aim of these deceptive investigations was to examine the accuracy in which psychiatrists could diagnose mental illnesses by attempting to have psychologically healthy people granted admission for rehabilitation. Resultantly, Rosenhan found that psychiatrists would typically diagnose anybody complaining of seemingly mild symptoms with serious mental illnesses, thus supporting the theory that mental illnesses are socially constructed and cannot be physically studied by anyone.

Fortifying the assertion that quantitative measurements of health are futile is the evidenced success of qualitative medical solutions. The mysticism of more personalistic and therapeutic approaches to the treatment of human well-being is phenomenally noticed to calm patients through remedies like hypnosis and meditation. Thus, the scientific method in medicine is incapable of explaining for all that visibly heals. Moreover, psychotherapy is a heavily supported method of psychological treatment where a practitioner will ask a client questions that unearth repressed traumatic memories. Curiously, as the client's understanding of the roots of their psychological disorder gradually became clear, their symptoms likewise reduced over time. Since we cannot physically study the effects of psychotherapy nor the objectivity of cognitive illnesses, it cannot be classed as a scientific method of treatment. Nevertheless, it works.

Somatoform Disorders

A somatoform disorder is generally described as a psychological disorder that manifests physical symptoms devoid of a physical cause. They are typically caused by excessive cognitive desires tricking the rest of the body and cannot be empirically studied, treated with medicine targeting the physical symptoms, or ascribed to other medical conditions. An example of a somatoform disorder is a phantom pregnancy whereby women will develop the general symptoms of pregnancy after intense longing to be with a child, such as missing a monthly period during their menstrual cycle, a swollen belly, and feelings of nausea.

Due to the professional disagreement that they generate, somatoform disorders are a good illustration of the limitations of both qualitative and quantitative methods of medical research. In addition to the validity weaknesses outlined previously, reliability issues like ungeneralisable and potentially bias findings are clearly resultant of the case study and observational research methods that immeasurable subject matter like this depend on to be intellectually grasped.

Impersonal Treatment

The Western infatuation with the biomedical model of health disregards the importance of a person-centred approach to healthcare and only offers generic explanations and medications. Frustratingly, these overgeneralised prescriptions stupidly pay no heed to the incomprehensibility complex nature of personal individuality and are often very ineffective. For example, a naïvely impersonal practitioner may administer the exact same method of treatment to one service user who is comfortable with this treatment, and another who is not. Clearly, the uncomfortable service user is more likely to be incompliant and may resist treatment. This client-practitioner conflict destroys the function of the treatment, but the adoption of a more person-centred approach will ensure treatment is tailored to a client's personal values and will inevitably be more helpful to them.

 Humanistic psychologist Carl Rogers fathered the client-centred therapy whereby people can be encouraged to self-actualise their ideal self-images in an accepting, empathetic, and genuine environment. The person-centred approach, which is a development of client-centred therapy, encourages service users to further their eternally compassionate human nature and subjective understanding of themselves as only they have the ability to understand their own mental processes. Whilst a degree of the humanistic approach to psychological treatment is evidenced in humanistic psychotherapy and person-centred care plans within some residential healthcare facilities, the vast majority of modern medicine rides the biomedical model. Psychologically, cognitive behavioural therapy (CBT) is condemned for its disregard for the possible roots of an individual's mental health issues and has often been noted to make service users feel hopeless and unimportant.

Overmedicalisation

Across most of the First World, it is plainly obvious that medical diagnoses brand those who live with them. For instance, the negative social connotations of being labelled 'autistic' in the normative West opens these service users up to being bullied, something continuous seen to occur both on online social media platforms and in person at school. Additionally, this overmedicalisation so obviously fortifies the social stigma of living on the autism spectrum that it is nearly impossible for an 'autist' to become steadily employed, irrespective of their thankfully recognised savant-like gifts that could skilfully assist in many professions. Appallingly, this overmedicalisation will always relegate a person to a patient. However, in Scandinavia, a person living with autism is not considered to be suffering from a medical condition. Rather, they are progressively seen to possess a different personality, just like every other human being.

Societal deviance is increasingly being medicalised. To expand, a person who engages in particular behaviour deemed to be culturally abnormal is subjected to medical jurisdiction such as the repetitive personal choice of gambling eventually being labelled as an addiction. Of course, there is a biochemical element of excessive dopamine production during the undertaking of these addictive actions, a but medicalisation it comes at the counterproductive cost of lowering the self-esteem of others. Also, the medicalisation of deviance conjures a dangerous precedent in criminality that paves the way for further healthcare threats. For example, dangerous criminals have an amazingly easy option to legally plead insanity to escape incarceration which somewhat decreases the incentive for potential offenders to avoid committing violent crimes as they know their punishment could be weak.

Iatrogenesis

Bizarrely, the side effects of medications prescribed for people diagnosed with a disease or illness are commonly worse than their original symptoms. Such as with sertraline, patients suffering from a spell of depression and anxiety will usually feel drowsy as a result of their demoralised state of mind, yet once a person takes a dose of an antidepressant, like sertraline, they then often claim to feel extremely fatigued, meaning that the prescribed medication has strengthened a patient's symptoms. Similarly, women who are taking birth control pills will experience excruciating groin pain and sickness. So, who decides what feelings are unhealthy and why is modern medicine permeating with ridiculous side effects? Well, one simple explanation is, of course, that each medication performs a specific function and that side effects are just excusable collateral damage. Although, governmental sceptics agree on the conclusion that side effects are purposefully included and enhanced to scare away people who may want to rely on this medication to live with their condition and force people into more normative behaviour. Despite the heartfelt conspiracies of social justice at play in the former argument, it is difficult to believe that governmental order the artificially inclusion of side effects to discourage abnormal behaviour as the medication itself contrariwise encourages normative behaviour.

Rehabilitation

To attempt to mentally rehabilitate people encompassing the lowest categories of social positions is to cement a societal value of unconditional humanism; a human being that has contracted an illness that they cannot control should never be abandoned. Psychopaths, however (or sociopaths as they are more incorrectly referred to by out of touch morons), are people living with antisocial personality disorder (ASPD) who are treated like absolute vermin in every corner of Western medicine. Lazily, as soon as they are diagnosed of innocently carrying an inability to process empathetic thoughts outside of their own control, they are celebratorily locked in psychiatric wards like feral beasts. These heinous methods of confinement only accomplish the sending of a disgustingly inhumane message exemplifying the impossibility of self-improvement the way of their cell-dwelling patients. It is ridiculous that the individual virtuous capabilities beyond a lack of empathy that cannot be controlled are utterly ignored; it is ridiculous that people are characterised by mental illnesses that determine whether or not their livelihoods are worthy of saving.

Instead of helping them to retain the chance of rising to a functioning member of society, people living with ASPD are treated like monsters. In fact, they are treated so monstrously within the uncaring healthcare sector that their atrocious characterisation becomes a self-fulfilling prophecy and that inflicts pain upon the blameless recipient's identity and level of passion to drive towards their life goals. Collaterally, the oppressive maltreatment of some psychiatric patients normalises a dehumanising cultural perception of them through the example of their deindividualisation. Obviously, mental illnesses do not control the life choices that people have the ability to complete, but they have shown to limit the life opportunities they are given. Instead, a progressive society should strive to assess individuals' personal capacities on a case by case basis to unlock the truly equitable foundations of humanistic healthcare in society.

<u>Legislation</u>

Legislatively, British people living with mental and physical disorders have their chances of cultural assimilation boosted by the *Equality Act 2010* that defines disability as a protected characteristic by which targeted discrimination against is outlawed. However, this reassimilation would never be required if disabled people were not already cited as social outcasts. Moreover, whilst the Mental Capacity Act 2005 ensures that the personal choices and informed decisions of cognitively impaired individuals are valued with the deprivation of liberty amendment, but it systematically fails to alter the plagues of social stigma stemming from the actions and inactions of national governments that is still evidenced today.

Health and Social Care

The Western sectors of health and social care (excluding Scandinavia), based upon the narrow-mindedness of the biomedical model of health, fail to qualitatively address the intricacies of the human mind. Perhaps typifying the state of biomedical healthcare, social care is not looked at as a form of healthcare, but rather as an entirely separate entity. As a consequence, the social aspect of health is all but forgotten.

Foolishly, Western medications overzealously rely on the scientific method in analysis of problems unsolvable by the natural world which they transcend. Furthermore, the lack of suitable medical prescriptions allows for the further development of all medical issues, especially threats to personal mental well-being in the form of biomedically untreatable mental illnesses, which are socially constructed by the deterministically uncaring society in which they are inherent. How can the West claim to be saving lives with science when it simultaneously kills citizens via its own societal constructs? There are no cures for all ills; there are only more ills.

Chapter Fifteen: Individuality - A

What is Individuality?

Every single person in the world is distinguished from one another by a plethora of personal characteristics: appearances, behaviours, beliefs, influences, memories, personalities, styles, and values are all small examples of what sets people apart, indications of what makes them individual. Although, individuality itself stands alone as an existentially holistic phenomenon that mere words cannot describe, nor the human mind comprehend. If the treasured reader is to take any uncomplicated message from this chapter, let it be this: everyone is different. Indeed, everybody is different, yet a painfully reductionistic worldview is currently hounding the sad, sad West, lessening any importance placed on individuals and centring cultures and groups at their expense. Today, people are characterised by singular attributes or labels, a process that is not only immoral, but also bafflingly stupid. Again, people are different, therefore any attempt to understand another person on the basis of social and physical characteristics, rather than their own expressions, will simply fall victim to an overzealous generalisation that renders such opinions invalid.

Conversely, adopting an empathetic method of thinking will allow an open-minded person to better appreciate a subject's life-happenings, but still not fully understand them. What is individuality? Well... who knows?

Despite the enigmatic reality of individuality, value in its consideration remains an ever-important aspect in the promotion of individual mental wellness. To demonstrate true respect for another individual when first meeting them, one must try to remove all pre-existing opinions of that person. If one can manage that in preparation for interpersonal scenarios, then they can systematically eliminate their own biases and begin their steps in taking a person-centred approach to conversation, making any recipient feel valued in the process. Secondly, one should attempt to empathise with the other person, considering what personal factors may have influenced their current perspectives. Empathetic thinking will increase the likelihood of a mutual understanding, developing the grounds for civil and receptive conversation. Finally and perhaps most prominently, one must take a holistic view of any person they may be talking to, considering everything that they know (or at least can rationally conceive) about that person, in order to make the most well-informed decisions about their behaviour and what to say on the basis of the person's beliefs, mannerisms, and social backgrounds amongst others things, but should simultaneously avoid fundamentally characterising them based on these characteristics, as such a thing would jeopardise the purpose of holism.

Let it be known to all readers, that the most venomous of actions one could possibly undertake against the interests of any individual is to engage an oversimplistic generalisation of their beliefs or values and proceed to characterise them in accordance with this atrocity. Alas, this is not an unpopular tendency of the Western populous, who consistently portray those they dislike as walking endorsements of any 'straw-manned', undesirable views they are said to behold. This heinous act of vilification is the bane of collective happiness; overgeneralisation of particular characteristics that may or may not even be present in a person is an attack on self-security that must be quenched, and it can only be done so if everyone is taught to take a person-centred approach towards each other by the highest societal authorities.

Exploring Individuality: Psychopathology

Although individuals cannot be defined by any mental disorders that they live with, comparing and contrasting the different psychological perspectives' psychopathological explanations for the development of mental health issues is certainly a useful way of analysing their approaches to individuality. Since behaviourism and psychodynamics have been covered throughout large portions of this text thus far, both the biological and cognitive approaches will instead be described and evaluated against humanistic theories of psychopathology.

Biologists in psychology attempt to explain the roots of mental health issues completely by way of genetic inheritance, brain damage, and evolution. For example, psychologists championing the biological approach suggest that schizophrenia is a genetically inherited chronic mental illness that can have evidence of its confliction supported by the observation of enlarged left-sided ventricles in the 'sufferer's' brain. The biologist would continue to build their genetic account by stating that schizophrenia is seen in almost half of identical twins. Additionally, they claim that phobias are wired into people are a result of evolution, specifically, a person living with arachnophobia (an irrational fear of spiders) must have had risk-averse ancestors that would recognise the danger venomous spiders posed to their health and would run away. Historically, these fears played a large part in natural selection, and evolutionary psychologists claim that they are passed down generation by generation, forming phobias. Overall, the biological approach perpetuates the idea that all mental health issues are resultant of conditions that can be physically researched using the scientific method, rather than through theoretical consideration of environmental and social influences.

Psychologists adopting the cognitive approach, such as Aaron Beck and Albert Ellis, claim that people become anxious or depressed because they believe that they are vulnerable to anxiety or depression because of an external happening, rather than developing these disorders because of any direct impacts on their wellness due to external happenings. They, amongst other cognitive psychologists, express the view that cognitive distortions such as selective attention (seeing only the negative feature of an event), magnification (exaggerating the importance of undesirable events), overgeneralisation (drawing negative conclusions from single, insignificant events), and illogical thought patterns (self-defeating cognitions that can plunge someone into a spiral of overthinking) cause negative memory biases in a person, eating their self-esteem and leaving them vulnerable to the emergence anxiety, depression, or other disorders. In particular, the cognitive approach provides three negative thought patterns, seen in individuals with low self-esteem, that it uses to explain the symptomatic behaviours in people living with OCD: hyper-vigilance (sufferers always search for sources of the problems), catastrophic misinterpretation (irrational ideas concerning unfortunate consequences if rituals are not performed), and memory problems (poor memory for basic actions, causing them to repeat actions like washing their hands). In addition to this, the cognitive triad, an interacting model of negative cognitions, is applied to the justification of the cognitions of people living with mood disorders, those being a repetitive cycle of negative views about oneself, the world, and the future. To elaborate, cognitive psychologists classify 'sufferers' of mental illnesses by their negative thought processes, referred to as cognitions, whilst upholding the belief that people can be diagnosed with mental disorders through speculation of their respective thought patterns. Humanistic psychology, drawn from the philosophical stance of humanism, the inquiry of existentialism, and the study of phenomenology, is an approach to psychology that empathises both the individual's natural and spiritual pursuit of self-actualisation, a realisation of personal potential inspired by Abraham Maslow's hierarchy of needs. Maslow's hierarchy of needs, specifically, is a motivational model of human development and needs holding true that individuals have five different fulfilment urges that they must systemically meet in order to reach their full potential. Physiological needs, the first and most prominent of the two material basic needs, sits at the bottom of the hierarchy, encompassing the dietary, environmental, and sleep requirements to maintaining good physical health. Secondly, the final basic need of safety involves the maintenance of security in a person's life, including financial stability and job or housing security. Just above safety, the first human psychological need of love and belonging, dependant on the formation and retainment of emotional attachments such as friendships and intimate relationships. Next, esteem makes up the latter half of Maslow's human psychological needs, meaning that everyone needs to feel a personal sense of prestige and accomplishment before they can satisfy the former need of self-fulfilment, self-actualisation. Neither a material nor a psychological need, self-actualisation can only be met when an individual becomes the self that they are capable realising in every aspect, including that in the senses of psychology and spirituality: although wholly uncommitted to celestial mysticism, the deepest desire of their fundamentally human soul together with an acting acceptance of their extraordinary place, perhaps even destiny, in the ambient world; it is when they truly become the best version of themself.

Humanistic psychologists believe that human beings are born to be their best selves, but the world is pushing them down. Being rejected for a job, for example, is an environmental factor that causes low self-esteem in some individuals. Consequently, vulnerable, a person with low self-esteem might develop anxiety, mood, or personality disorders that prey on their poor sense of personal security, or a direct deprivation of one of Maslow's psychological needs, 'esteem'. Moreover, American humanistic psychologist and psychotherapist Carl Rogers wanted his clients to ask themselves 'who am I?' so they might learn to better understand themselves on their path the self-actualisation (it should be noted that Rogers, whilst he was still inspired by his work, used a different model of personal motivation to Maslow that saw self-actualisation as a fundamental part of human development, rather than an ultimate goal that only a scarce few achieved). Through consideration of their own self-concepts, clients could begin to clearly distinguish their ideal self from their real self and begin to congregate the two. Rogers believed that psychological disorders could be resultant of a failure to self-actualise, therefore achieving a mindful interconnection of their ideal self and real self via a state of congruence could finally unlock the gates of self-actualisation as they would unravel their mysteries of the 'self', something that only they have the ability to do. Additionally, Rogers thought that individuals with mental health difficulties must take a holistic view of the self in order to comprehend the problems they encounter, exploring exactly what has gone wrong, when and where it went wrong, and how it has affected their well-being. As a psychotherapist, he founded his signature therapeutic approach, originally call client-centred therapy, a process which has now revolutionised the health and social care sector today with practitioners adopting the newly developed person-centred approach in the formulation of individually tailored service plans that work within a client's beliefs, preferences, and values in order to assure their comfort, maximise their self-worth, and increase their likelihood of compliance with care that remains in their best interests, without depriving them of their liberty. Lastly, on the importance of psychotherapy, Rogers claimed that a client could be cure by a therapist who embraces three essential traits: avoid being judgemental, demonstrate accurate empathy, and be genuine.

The biological approach to psychology truly exemplifies the intellectual brilliance of the scientific method, an empirical process of acquiring knowledge of the natural world that has inspired revolutionising intellectual and philosophical movements, such as the Age of Enlightenment for the progressive development of entire civilisations. Through the scientific method, biologists understand that certain mental health conditions can and have been caused by damage to corresponding areas of the brain through careful and repetitive observation of physical cause and effect relationships, thus universally defining this as a scientific fact. For example, the now generalisable case of nineteenth-century railroad foreman Phineas Gage indicated that different areas of the brain held different cognitive functions and that localised damage to these parts caused respective cognitive dysfunctions. Granted, there is much controversy surrounding the reliability of reports around Gage's prior behaviour, but events following this incident have only supported the scientific claims of localised brain functions and what effects localised damage has on a subject's mental health.

Notwithstanding the biological approaches generally incredible heights of research reliability, it systematically fails to address its own invalidity issue and reductionist worldview, for its shallow research is so often narrowed by utter ignorance of social and environmental factors. The genetic explanation for schizophrenia, in particular, has to be fallacious as schizophrenia must be observed in both monozygotic twins to draw a rational biological conclusion, instead, the biological approach jumps to conclusions based on painfully little evidence (genetic influence is also something that scientists do not yet understand), and inadvertently lends support to the social learning theory, as the psychotic disorder is more commonly seen in households with history of the condition, but not always more so. Conceivably, biological psychologists, behavioural neuroscientists, or whatever they wish to call themselves, are continuously drawing conclusions entirely from assumptions, something of a paradox to the rationality they hold so dear.

Additionally, the biological approach poses both logical and moral dilemmas in its propagation of determinism. Despite the complexity of genetic influence not being fully understood, it is held true that the son of an alcoholic father is almost genetically destined to repeat their father's abusive behaviour, spitting in the face of free will. Should the further explanation of this absurdity of this idea be required, both ethics and theology can be used as an elaborate tool to do so. Morality, a concept that can be rationally concluded to exist in some ways, is metaphysical, therefore objective moral values cannot be accounted for by the scientific method. To mirror a thought-provoking apologetic argument, if an omnipresent, omniscient, and ultimately necessary force that is simultaneously immanent and transcendent does not exist (God?), then objective moral values cannot exist? However, integral to the Age of Enlightenment, moral philosopher Immanuel Kant argued that a sense of dualistic sense of morality is innately present in all people, and from this it should be concluded that objective moral values must exist, therefore the necessary force must exist, logically proving that free will exists. Hence, the biological approach cannot use deterministic explanations for mental health issues, or define people as such, nor can it misuse Darwin's amazing theory of evolution to presume naturalistic reason for the existence of an innate sense of morality in humans for the aforementioned problems of strange phobias, which play no part in natural selection in accordance with evolutionary theory.

The cognitive approach, which thankfully demands much less extensive critical evaluation, is similar to its biological rival in that its psychopathological theories are too assumption based, simplistic, and unspecific, in addition to offering both ungeneralisable and unquantifiable explanations for all mental health difficulties, albeit for very different reasons. The cognitive triad, for instance, is a flagship of cognitive psychopathology that assumes mental health issues arise in individuals exclusively following a cycle of three negative thought patterns. Clearly, this is a very limited idea that neglects the plethora of alternative causes for mental disorders.

Moreover, through the cognitive perspective, one must relegate the complexity of the human mind by viewing it as functioning much like a computer, simply processing inputted information. Obviously, the human brain does not function like a computer, for computers can have their memories physically contorted and examined, whilst cognitive memory is not physical at all and (despite the brilliant technological developments in science) cannot be physically studied. The 'cognition' of computers is all a visible process that has quite literally been designed by human beings; the inner workings of the human mind are all but entirely impossible to physically study and can only have its mysteries speculated upon. There is no way of proving that the external world is even real, how can one possibly attempt to measure the reality of cognition beyond metaphysical guesswork?

On evaluation of the validity and reliability of the humanistic approach to psychopathology, one must accept that large parts of the psychological perspective are utterly dependent on a level of overoptimism and faith that borders on naivety. To illustrate, Rogers' theory of the three necessary characteristics of a good therapist lack any technical methods of psychotherapy needed in order to 'improve' the behaviour in most clients, despite his three characteristics still being critical in achieving that. So, whilst these traits are fundamentally needed in order to inspire a change in the behaviour of a client via psychotherapy, they are usually not enough to achieve 'effective' therapy.

However, despite the many theoretical shortcomings of the humanistic approach, it remains the safest practical method of effective psychotherapy, and the most rational in its psychopathological explanations. This is because the only thing that psychology proves is that human minds and behaviours are either too complex or immeasurable to fully understand, therefore the minds or behaviours of other people simply cannot be comprehended, and that the closest therapists can get to understanding a client in order to help them is through the person-centred approach. By utilising empathic thinking, a therapist adopting a person-centred view of their client, considering their whole life experiences, values, and more, will have a better chance of discovering constructive solutions to a client's problems, who are now much more receptive now that they have been used as a vital source of expert information about the topic at hand, themself, say unlike behaviourists who only look at presently expressed behaviour and ignore all other contributing factors from a 'patient's' past when slackly diagnosing them.

Plainly, the humanistic approach to psychopathology assists psychology to better understand individual people and accurately identify problems with the self. For wherever this approach is not taken, for example, ineffective treatment is chosen by uninformed practitioners and further damage is potentially done to the mental stability and welfare of individual clients. Therefore, humanism is by far and wide the safest and most rational approach to psychopathology, whilst being the only perspective that even scratches the elusive surface of what makes the individual unique.

Traditional Humanism and Contemporary Transpersonal Psychology

Traditional humanism, the form of humanism analysed under the last subtitle, is very similar to a more contemporary humanistic psychology known as transpersonal psychology. Like the traditional humanists Maslow and Rogers, transpersonal psychologists look beyond the limits to the most primitive structures of Maslow's hierarchy of needs for answers to what a person might do once they have achieved self-actualisation, in an attempt to expand studies and, thus, beliefs about the supreme potential for human development. This is where the idea of self-transcendence was conceived, a new final stage of human development, which is basically an idea that humans must rise beyond physical and personally spiritual accomplishments in order to reach their full potential, which is unbound by personal desires that bare the destructive potential to stimulate grandiose egos. Self-transcendence, however, is far from a basic idea; its true meaning cannot be relegated a description found in one sentence. Rather, to achieve self-transcendence is to overcome both the physical and spiritual limits of individual potential; it means to transcend the metaphysical shackles of phenomenological desires; it perpetuates the necessity to understand one's ethereal place in a material world, and accept such peripheral phenomena as fundamentally factual. Ultimately, to self-transcend might be to see the world for how it truly is, devoid of subjective interventions, but one can only do these via a process that is agonisingly intellectual, through incomprehensible volumes of fortitude, knowledge, and willpower.

Maslow, who first created the concept of self-transcendence, held that interpretative factors such as memory could never be scientifically accounted for, therefore only through the humanistic perspective can human consciousness be studied. This leads to the illogical yet scientific tendency to draw conclusions after ignoring any immaterial factors, which is perhaps reason for Maslow's view describing how the ideological consequences of the scientific worldview are deeply, intellectually unsatisfying.

On his hierarchy of needs, Maslow was resolute in his absolution that no person could climb the hierarchy without having satisfied all of the needs prior. So, for example, a person who has not attended to their basic physiological needs would not be able to self-actualise or even develop a good sense of self-esteem through making benevolent choices. Maybe Maslow's reasoning here stems from the reasonable faith that it is hard to care about qualities like virtue and humility when a person is hungry in every aspect of life.

Crucial to Rogers' favoured therapeutic approach, client-centred therapy, was the need for therapists to empathise with the client using unconditional positive regard (UPR). Interlocking all three of Rogers' principles for effective psychotherapy: being empathetic, genuine, and non-judgemental, UPR sets an altruistic atmosphere for empowering conversation for the client as they are constantly accepted by the therapist for who they are. Rogers, to illustrate, would always offer clients compassion even when they had done something wrong, reassuring them that they are not defined by the mistakes they make in life. Being met with this passive acceptance was often uncommon for clients, who were previously heavily judged by their few actions to such a point whereby they eventually felt characterised by them, so Rogers' positivity would in turn raise their demolished self-esteems and motivate them to personally develop. By UPR, Rogers taught the psychological community that the unsympathetic belittlement of others is a primary cause for their unhappiness, and that with emotional acceptance and support, one could give another the hope they need to change their life.

As previously discussed, Rogers' theory of the three fundamental characteristics of an effective therapist is insufficient by today's standards, although they do still remain crucial aspects of efficient psychotherapy. Together with the use of UPR however, empathetic, genuine, non-judgemental psychotherapists can avoid setting restrictive demand characteristics via their encouragement of clients to explore their own free-will in the journey of self-improvement, especially as the inherently humanistic atmosphere of their therapy sessions helps clients to feel safe and supported, unlike the so-called 'patients' who are belittled by other psychotherapists who position themselves above them. For example, radical behaviourist psychotherapists only examine the behaviour that their 'patients' are expressing and jump to medical conclusions based on such little evidence, perhaps labelling people with disorders that they are not 'suffering' from. Transpersonal psychotherapists include the behaviour of clients when drawing out a holistic service plan for the purpose of good ecological validity, but do not reduce their view of a client only to that which their behaviour indicates.

Rogers also suggested that a person looking to achieve self-actualisation or transcendence must be in a state of congruence, as previously stated. What is interesting, though, is that Rogers believed this process could be greatly accelerated within therapy sessions held by genuine practitioners, the therapists respected clients enough to always tell them the truth, or at least not to lie to them for any professional reason. The traditional humanist proposed that the truth heals people, a profoundly deep idea by which Western civilisation is actually founded upon; honesty was truly the best policy for Rogers. To apply his idea to a real-world setting,

Rogers would have thought that a relationship whereby couples took comfort in deceit were dysfunctional and toxic as they could not bear to face each other truthfully for fear of conflict. In all senses, real relationships are therapeutic, not primate dominance hierarchy disputes.

Rogers was a phenomenologist, he subscribed to the idea that data should be collected through qualitative means, through individual case studies, for example. Phenomenology, specifically, is the philosophical model of 'being', as well as the psychological study of subjective experience. Phenomenologists like Rogers believe that as one can only ever experience events from their own perspective, other people's experiences are in turn rendered incomprehensible. In fact, some radical phenomenologists view the differences in how people process information as so existential that spending a mere second in the life of another would cause one to go insane. Granted, this is an extremist view that is typically only raised by existential phenomenologists rather than, say, transpersonal psychologists, but there are important similarities between the fields nonetheless.

Phenomenology is closely linked to metaphysics, the philosophy of immaterial concepts and the relationships between them, such as with mind and matter. Aside from baring an odd-sounding job title, metaphysicians often question the reality of the external world, as they conceive that there is no logical proof that anything physically exists. To elaborate, concerned with metaphysics, some phenomenologists question whether or not the five senses provide a reliable sense of truth; they pose a question for which any answer must be considered a logical fallacy, as we cannot overgeneralise the collective significance of subjective experience, to do so would be scientifically unreliable. However, this is simply further reason to question why one would be attempting to combine quantitative science with qualitative humanism. Ultimately, if one thing is certain here it is that phenomenology is fundamental in underlining the importance of three notions: that empathising with others is an incredibly difficult, but absolutely necessary to appreciate what they might be experiencing, that one individual could never fully understand another, in fact, it is probably impossible to fully comprehend oneself, and finally that life's first-person experiences cause people to see what they aim at, so they should be very vigilant in choosing where they aim.

Transpersonal psychology is largely interpreted as the purest contemporary variant of humanistic psychology regarding its philosophical loyalty to traditional humanism. Transpersonal psychologists believe that spiritual aspiration drives the human psyche and is integral to its functional integration of the self's many aspects. Transpersonal psychology offers mostly the same psychopathological explanations of individuality as the likes of Maslow and Rogers, concurring that human's physical bodies suppress their soul's potential and that wholeness helps people understand themselves. Except that, contemporarily, psychologists must account for every single aspect of human life, including of all its cultural, physical, spiritual, and other components beyond the personal psych, as transpersonal literally means to examine consciousness transcending both individual minds and the physical world. Additionally, all life experiences are considered potentially growth-enhancing to the transpersonal psychologist, who, just like the legendary humanistic psychologists, suggest that in order to become the powerful vessels that they are destined to become, humans must self-transcend and escape the mundaneness of worldly happenings and that the fundamental spiritual aspects of the self cannot be ignored, as they so often are.

Chapter Sixteen: Individuality - B

Existential Psychology: Existentialism

Existential psychology unsurprisingly hinges on the aptly named philosophical movement known as existentialism. Existentialism is concerned with the purpose of life and what can give an individual's life meaning. Similar to nihilists, existentialists believe that life has no inherent meaning, such as a personal destiny or a fundamental fate, although they also believe that every individual is tasked with finding a purpose for their own life, according to their own values, thus deviating from nihilism. Today, existential thinking has heavily influenced how important many psychologists view empathetic thinking, as many people now live their lives well within accordance with their own moral paradigm, something that both existential and other contemporarily humanistic psychologists believe should be considered in order to understand the behaviour of a respective client.

Dubbed the father of existentialism, enlightened Danish philosopher Soren Kierkegaard (1813-1855) is regarded as the first existentialist philosopher. Before forming views consistent with the aforementioned, he became so disassociated with the social constraints of his native society that he completely deviated from them, rejecting their shared norms and values and, following an existential crisis as a teenager, began living his life according to his own. However, Kierkegaard would find that expressing one's individuality was not so easy in a society that so potently oppresses its population through listless measures of social control. Targeting the Danish state church, for example, Kierkegaard claimed that his beloved faith was being manipulated by state authorities for the purpose of maintaining societal order, in addition to encouraging a sort of 'lazy' religion that contradicts its true beauty. In elaboration, Kierkegaard hated society and all of its components; he believed that civilisation was almost doomed to live a life of tragic conformity and that all who are prevented from being themselves are bound to endlessly despair. How times change…

Before thinking about the existentialist approach to purpose, one must first consider how existentialists view the properties of existing objects. Ancient Greek philosophers Plato and Aristotle conceived that an object's set of core properties are necessary for that object to be what it is and they named these properties an 'essence'. They theorised that a human's essence is present before their birth and that, in order to live a good life, one must live in adherence to their essence, or what could be argued to be their destiny, thus forming the theory of essentialism. Now, essentialism is actually incompatible with existentialism as the latter pronounces that existence really precedes essence, so one determines who they are, creates their own destinies, and gives their own life individual purpose through the way they choose to live, rather than having a predetermined purpose.

Despite its vigorous attack on spiritual concepts such as destiny and theological determinism, existentialism is not mutually exclusive to theism (see Kierkegaard). Of course, they refute teleology by their insistence that the world was created devoid of purpose and that purpose is individually constructed, but they might be indifferent to

apologetics arguing for the existence of God via the kalam cosmological argument, such as the respected Christian theologian William Lane Craig, who popularised the ancient theological defence by restating three simple but hitherto irrefutable points:
1. Whatever begins to exist has a cause.
2. The universe began to exist.
3. Therefore, the universe has a cause.

As the kalam cosmological argument has teleological elements, theist existentialists can occasionally be seen endorsing it.

Whilst existentialism poses a philosophical problem for some believers, it is equally not nihilistic, as nihilism is a reductionist movement that stands unrelated to ethics, but simultaneously concerned with morality itself. To expand on this point, nihilism reduces the angst (a fear of human freedom and responsibility) as reason for an inexistence of objective grounds for moral action, rather than objective grounds for action. Kierkegaard, for example, insists that religious morality suspends ethics as the ethereal truths found in religion are infinite, whereas the philosophy of humans, like nihilism, is finite. Culturally speaking, existentialists characteristically persist through the absurd, a plain in which nihilists would eternally dwell.

According to Kierkegaard, humans are creatures that rely on meaning, yet they are born into the absurd, the state of existence in a meaningless world and self. Absurdity, to existentialists, is the search for answers in an answerless world. With these things considered, Kierkegaard caustically laughs at Western civilisation, which is scattered with individuals who collectively cry out for answers and receive, yet continue to cry anyway. This is his definition of absurdity.

In response to Maslow's hierarchy of needs, both classical and contemporary existentialists criticise the apparently flawed template of human motivation for assuming the level of importance of all human needs, utterly devoid of consideration for how the values of individuals may fluctuate from person-to-person. For example, a minimum-wage dependant worker might still give up work to fulfil their self-image as a full-time social media influencer, willingly neglecting the physiological needs in favour of their psychological needs yet still finding happiness and fulfilment. Nonetheless, everyone's individual hierarchy of needs cannot be known because everyone maintains their own values and a respective intensity of integrity for said values. On criticisms of the psychology of the hierarchy of needs, existentialists make two more key points: that different individuals are motivated by different things, and that people's motivations are acting simultaneously at different volumes so analysing them is practically impossible. Overall, there is no simplistic overarching explanation for human motivation because humans are complex creatures.

Through the existential eye, one must perceive that as there are no guidelines for human actions, humans are forced to design their own moral codes, however, humans will inevitably behave in ways that are inherently inconsistent with each of their moral codes, therefore, the subsequent states of chaos will surely lead to tragic events. This is the reality of radical freedom. Jean-Paul Sartre, an early nineteenth-century French philosopher, playwright, and political activist, was a key figure in the philosophies of both existentialism and phenomenology. He famously claimed that "we are condemned to be free", also suggesting that nobody can live authentically considering the absurd. Sartre understood that the difficulties a person encounters must be resolved by themselves, otherwise another's answer to their question will be inauthentic. To live according to the principles established by others is dubbed bad faith, it is burying your head in the sand against the absurd and becoming a sheep. If one wishes to live an authentic life, then it is absolutely necessary that they choose a path set in accordance with their own values, taught to them through their own experiences and morality, factors unbeknownst to any other. As Sartre concludes, regardless of its consequence, an individual's authentic choice will always be the correct choice as it is founded upon values specific to themselves.

Thinking back to Kierkegaard, he would scornfully mock the real world that so easily convinces its naïve civilisation that the joys of life are nothing but lazy, tedious, and unambitious 'nothings' written for a conformist society to anguish in chasing that might even be instantaneously unobtainable. However, Kierkegaard also offered a positive outlook on life when he implored that one could (and should) imbue life with whatever purpose they want. Life does not have to be meaningless forever. What is especially empowering about this is that it means nobody can tell one that their life is not worth anything, say, if one does not follow a lucrative career path or does not have children. One's life purpose is whatever they so choose, therefore only they possess the ability to choose what that worthy purpose is.

Much like Sartre once said, the world will never be filled with elements of justice or order unless these elements, which are individually constructed, are perceived into society by the self. If not, then society will forever remain unjust, according to that self.

Existential Psychology: The Enigma of Individuality

Individuality is enigmatic; the deep-rooted components of the self's essence are, quite literally, inconceivable to other people. To elaborate, the following chronological points are listed in attempting to explain the roots of individuality:

- Genetic predispositions to the development of personalities.

- Primary socialisation and other influential interpersonal relationships.
- Unquantifiable amounts of specific experiences known only to the subject.
- Endless interpretations that are biologically and socially influenced by an individual's unmatchable individuality.
- Years of further cognitive development, growing more and more unique.
- Can never know what someone else is thinking.
- Cannot understand their experiences.
- External judgement biases and limitations consequent of the judge's individuality.

The case for proving the enigmatic reality of individuality is easily provided through its obvious theoretical validity and reliable strengths made apparent by the endorsements of various psychological perspectives. From existentialist thinking even to theories of biological determinism, classical behaviourism, and psychoanalysis, achieving absolute empathy must be impossible as one's brain cannot comprehend the life of another person. Individuals are too attuned to their own world. People should ask themselves, "what do I actually notice about other people?" In most cases, the honest answer would be "to little to make an informed decision about my opinion on them", thus, it is most rational to simply listen to others in a non-judgemental way, much like Rogers proposed, as you will probably never understand there essence anyway.

In light of the enigmatic reality of individuality, people who believe that some opinions are really objective truths, such as overgeneralising people who say that some statements can be universally offensive, should be embarrassed with their revering of logical fallacies.

Again, opinions of what is and is not offensive are founded upon insurmountable aspects of the self and the morality of the self, they are born of values formed over a million moments atop an already unique mind. To determine the ultimate correctness of behaviour, one must be an omniscient deity, not a random person from Stoke-on-Trent, say.

Existential Psychology: The Self is Unknowable

How can one truly understand themselves? As even reiterated by psychoanalyst Carl Jung, the self is unknowable due to the unconscious factors that rule the individual mind. The human brain is not flawless. A person's memory, for instance, cannot account for their unconscious cognitions and repressed feelings, which both influence their personal mindset and set them apart from others. Furthermore, a person with low self-esteem might be beating themselves up about their own self-image, but this itself is a multiple failure in logic as this person will overexaggerate this importance of something that they cannot know and, thus, they will overgeneralise its supposed meaning (this also integrates cognitive psychological theory into existential psychology). With all things considered, one should really look to unconditional positive regard on the path to self-respect; using Rogers' approach to view the self is not only more rational than condemning one's own actions, but it will surely lead to a happier life.

In respect to the enigma of individuality, if one cannot know themselves, then others cannot know them. The constant existential angst humans suffer from ensuring that they are never content, yet they cannot always be empathised with, helped, or have the exasperating enigmas of their mental health unravelled, alas eternalising the existential angst. Fittingly, Kierkegaard once proposed that, despite being lived forwards, life could only be understood backgrounds, thus highlighting the impossibility of avoiding angst and making sense of life's experiences. However, through self-reflection, one may one day scale their own mysteries and obtain a state of contentment.

Existential Psychology: Humanistic-Existential Psychology

As Sartre expressed, existential is of course a humanism, so humanistic-existential psychology is really no different from existential psychology, excusing some rather tedious and vague differences, such as a 'heavier' importance put upon a phenomenological approach. Anyway, humanistic-existential psychologists interest themselves with their clients' fear of their impending death and treat them using a person-centred approach that might consider the worth of a client building a legacy and finding meaning to combat desperation, depending on the client's values.

In Western society, existential psychologists recognise Kierkegaard's historic philosophy that Western society curses its citizenry with freedom. For Westerners, a complete freedom of choice results in a complete responsibility for the outcome, creating enormous pressure for people to make the correct choices, causing such societal anxiety that people resort to suicide, as supported by Durkheim's sociology.

The existential angst marks the individual's starting point in a journey of dreadful helplessness in an apparently meaningless world, an absurd world. Existential psychologists implore that in order to scale an existential crisis, one must first make peace with these anxieties and accept them as normal, which they are, of course.

To close this section on existential psychology, one should reflect, once again, on the work of Søren

Kierkegaard. Perhaps authentic meaning is created by the self, in the most complex and non-sensical of processes, so whether or not one makes a choice, know that the self will regret it either way.

Cross-Cultural Psychology

Cross-cultural psychology is a contemporary psychological perspective that analyses the differences in human behaviour across different cultures. Specifically, the approach studies how cultures influence human behaviour and how cultural barriers prevent humans from developing a healthy sense of self-security. For example, a transgender person living in Sweden may feel that they are accepted in society, whereas a Muslim living in Ireland might feel resented by the native population and will struggle to integrate or even assimilate into the culture. Cross-cultural psychopathologists propose that these cultural barriers cause mental health issues such as depression and anxiety.

Cross-cultural psychologists sometimes criticise Maslow's hierarchy of needs as it ignores cultures outside the West and view achievement as an ultimate goal, rather than, say, the psychological need of security which is the ultimate goal for some people in poorer countries. Of course, this is not that these people do not care about being poor, they might just care for security more than they do for great material wealth. However, Maslow might have argued that these people are stuck on that physiological need, therefore it would be illogical for them to climb the hierarchy and begin striving for the psychological need for esteem. Nonetheless, collective achievements may also be valued higher than individual ones in more tribalistic cultures, just as homeostasis may be valued higher in almost any country that is not Western.

Positive Psychology

What makes people thrive? What contributes to happiness? How is health benefitted by positive emotions? Which habits build emotional resilience? Positive clinical psychologists ask these questions to boost the self-image of their clients, ensuring their happiness through any means necessary. Critically, these practitioners also recognise that negative emotions lead to mental health issues. For example, a person failing to meet essential principles such as dignity and self-worth can cause this. Furthermore, depression is episodic and chronic and, whilst 'positive thinking' is far from a holistic cure, using positive psychological techniques to help an empowering environment can help a person build confidence. This is especially important for positive psychologists as they view that Western society will naturally push people down, so to speak.

Positive psychology is underpinned by the ethics of utilitarianism, conceivably for the worse, rather than the better, unfortunately. Founded by English philosopher and social reformer Jeremy Bentham, utilitarianism, the family of consequentialist ethical theories, claims that the morality of an action should be measured according to how much happiness it creates. In positive psychology, an aim is to maximise a client's happiness, so this theory is obviously very prominent. However, utilitarianism can only determine how the majority populous can be uplifted by actions, not everyone, because not everyone is content with the same things due to their ever-conflicting personal values. Therefore, practitioners should aim to increase happiness in a client by considering the adjudged morality of an action itself, using their own morality, as when faced with various conflicting moral paradigms, one can only trust in their own. Overall, the counter-productive overgeneralising practicality of consequentialist moral philosophy, such as Bentham's impractical utilitarianism, should be replaced by its superior ethical competitor, deontology, but provided that existentialist theory is integrated within it.

Providing (unintentional) support for positive psychology, behaviourists argue that because anxiety is learned and conditioned through experiences, it can also be unlearned. Humanists agree. According to positive psychologists, environmental factors contribute to how people feel, thus changing them can stimulate positive emotions. Interestingly, this is also the premise of CBT, whilst being conversely unsurprisingly relevant to PCT, provided that a person's individual strengths are considered that can help them be happier.

Sacrificing any need for further methodological evaluation, to conclude this section on positive psychology, an acronym will be provided below that represents the true meaning of the approach rather poetically:

P urpose
U nderstanding
R esponsibility
E njoyment

Kirk Schneider's Paradox Principle

Author and practising existential-humanistic psychotherapist Kirk J. Schneider implores that dogmatic thinking surrounding existential factors of existence leads to destructive behaviours and anxieties surrounding the apparent insignificance of life. Schneider also created the 'paradox principle', theorising that despite every human's inherent capacity for spirituality, autonomy, growth, uniqueness, and creativity, they also have a dark side that must be accepted and controlled. One must, therefore, acknowledge their flawed mind, which is split between good and evil, and reconcile their personal flaws, flaws that make them human.

Like Schneider, Dostoevsky can help people come to terms with their flaws, expressing that they are fundamental to human nature. For example, the Russian writer would reiterate that Jesus Christ's message and example is sound, but He is the son of God. Therefore humans should not suffer from shame when they fail to emulate Him. Nobody is divine; nobody is perfect.

Why is Individuality Overlooked?

Individuality is often overlooked in societies that are increasingly obsessed with globalism, thus socialism, thus collectivism. Collectivism is defined by the priority of societal welfare, over the welfare of the individuals within the society. Now, collectivists can claim that their movement, as it is, offers many socially progressive advantages. For example, people who are socialised into a collectivist society with collectivist ideals will be less selfish than if not, and the process of transition towards globalism (not globalisation) will focus on integrating marginalised social groups into society, contextualising their cultures, and protecting them from discrimination by soothing generalised behaviours about them, regardless on whether they are good or bad.

Obviously, collectivism has many theoretically limitations too. Since less weight is put on individual differences, people will have an enormous pre-expectation of correct behaviour and will probably react unsympathetically when a person deviates from such moral expectations. For instance, a radicalised child who becomes racist will have lacked the capacity to make informed decisions on their true ethical position as they are a child. However, collectivists would group these individuals as racists anyway, through the characterisation of their whole self on the basis of childhood mistakes, as they do not care for a person-centred approach to whether or not they are racist now, because labels are all that matter in a society that disregards the complexity of individual variation. Additionally, a paedophile who has served jail time, undergone probation, and been rehabilitated so as to reassimilate into society would still be labelled a 'pedo' following the completion of their sentence as the shared values of a collectivist society would disregard the individual potential for redemption and personal development in favour of severe punishment in accordance with socially constructed labels, an ironically right-wing view.

Individualism and Suicide

As covered in chapter eleven, Durkheim's theory of suicide consequent of capitalism highlights how individualism, rather than collectivism, can result in a devastating state of hopefulness, motivation, and emotional stability that will cause some people to prefer ending their lives than to subject themselves to a life of impossible competition, failure, and ridicule. However, existentialists can also help people realise how living by any sociological theory, whether it be left or right-wing, will prevent the individual from living their own life. Albert Camus, for example, once said that whatever steered one away from suicide was their individual meaning of life. Considering whatever any existentialists have said about the deindividualising nature of such an individualistic society, it is not difficult to understand why this is such a celebrated declaration.

Expanding on how individualism relates to psychopathology, capitalists societies have been criticised by social constructionists for applying stigma to behaviours through the systematic medicalisation of deviance, but this is not just behaviour that deviates from the shared norms and values of society. Also, it might be what challenges the functional hierarchy. For example, know that committing commonly used logical fallacies when arguing against capitalism, such as catastrophising the impact of an unimpactful event (see 'slippery slope'), leads to the perception that a person may have a cognitive impairment which psychiatrists might tick off as a symptom for schizophrenia under 'delusions', provided it is observed for at least one month. To socialists, this method of medicalising deviants is to force order; to conservatives, it is a method of protecting the delusional individual before attempting to cure them. Either way, the schizophrenic is likely to feel alienated from society and, in most cases, will suffer from depression that is arguable worse than their original symptoms (see chapter 14).

Individualism also has dire consequences for the collective attitude. For example, someone who is an attention seeker desperately looks for attention to have some sort of influence on others, like to make them laugh, or impress them. This is due to the competition infused into society by individualism. However, if one is proud of what they have achieved and has high self-security, then they will no longer endlessly try to impress others, or perhaps themselves. Simply put, people need to back themselves, for otherwise, society will definitely shoot them down.

Despair, Despair, Despair!

Dostoevsky famously said that people often do not realise their own qualities. They underestimate themselves and deplete their own self-image. To combat this, one must understand their strengths and set goals in accordance with them and their values. Then, one can achieve goals that they are proud of achieving and, provided their goals are set carefully enough, feel proud to reflect on one for the rest of their life. People should embrace what they are motivated by, of course they should. Though, can it really be all that simple?

According to Kierkegaard's wisdom, one hoping to achieve contentment in life cannot do so without having first completed a list of tasks in preparation for reaching such a position. Some of the steps to take are as follows:
- Disregard material possessions.
- Recognise that radical rationality is irrational.
- Accept your dissatisfaction with life.
- Love everyone.
- Take a leap of faith towards a silent God.

A qualitative leap, in his own words.

The Dane proposed that should a person fail to achieve these things, then they have no protection against the dehumanising social order which prevents maintenance of personal selfhood.

If one does not achieve selfhood, to become a self, then they will be stricken with a sickness of spirit and a lack of self. To achieve selfhood, one must relate opposing elements of human existence, such as the finite and the infinite, or the temporal and the eternal, thus solving the existential problem. If they fail, then, ultimately, they will be condemned to despair. Kierkegaard said that to despair is to suffer, but to suffer is to be human, so it is unavoidable and people will always despair at some stages in their lives. Specifically, to live in despair could be to subscribe to a subculture of rationalist materialism, ignoring the existence of human consciousness, that is fundamentally immaterial and spiritual, just as it is to meet human morality in a spiralling chasm of existential angst and despair. One may despair that they do not achieve the highs of their peers, but they may actually be despairing that they are not their ideal-self, and that their despair is the result of living the life of their true-self. Instead, one's own fundamental ambition must be discovered in their exploration of their subjective truths, once they have overcome despair by developing their own worldview, hence becoming their true self. Interestingly, such humanism may have served as some sort of inspiration for Rogers' theory of congruence in relation to self-actualisation, given their similarities.

Jungian theory conveys that people who do not make their unconscious motives conscious will have their life directed by them, a process which is sorely mistaken for fate, so often. Here, humanism can be combined with a tepid psychodynamic consideration of unconscious motives in a psychotherapeutic attempt to empathise with a person struggling to find their true self as, without total evaluation of a person's essence, no one can possibly hope to empathise with another.

If it is humanistic, then it is good, provided that it is also holistic.

Chapter Seventeen: Friendship

Authentic and Unauthentic Friendships

Authentic friendship is a true companionship; one can always count on their authentic friends to support them in their times of strife, at least as much as they can. An authentic friend group, to illustrate, must provide a supportive circle of trust. Of course, this is what friends are - other individuals in which one both provides and receives positively emotional company for and from, usually through frequent interpersonal communication. However, inauthentic friendships are toxic and do not provide such a bond, rather, they discourage them. In these 'friendships', a culture is created whereby certain or all members are taken advantage of through consistent ridicule or physical bullying to which they are unlikely to retaliate. Say, via peer pressure to pay for everything, or being excessively insulted behind their backs to an unnaturally great extent (this is because this is already a somewhat natural activity). Consequently, the toxicity that plagues these groups only results in the gradual relegation of the respective victims' self-esteem, and therefore their general happiness.

Tragically, a common trait of inauthentic friendships is a provisional lack of empathetic support, especially in relation to mental health or social issues. Inside these demonic circles, victims often feel isolated, and are vilified as attention-seekers by inauthentic friends, who are afflicted with an unawareness of the uncomplicated fact that mental illnesses prey on individuality, underlining the fundamentality of a person-centred approach, something people can provide simply by being empathic and by listening. Instead, these militant individuals would sooner ignore the disorderly individual's struggles in favour of bantering with the orderly group. An obvious point, yet also something that unfortunately must be taught, is that people (get this...) are different and they go through different difficulties differently, therefore they need to be treated differently. A person refusing to address someone else's problem because they perceive that their problem would be easier for them to deal with is just painfully stupid, do they really think that there is nothing that they find difficult in which the other person would interpret as a tedious task? One must ever remain humble in the face of another's suffrage, because should the roles be reversed, they would expect empathy and sympathy.

Like a sort of selfish therapist, some people hold that they are concerned with the welfare of their 'friends', but are too cognitively impaired to actually feel happy for, or to support, them. Like a spiteful toddler, perhaps they get jealous when their acquaintance's situation demands sympathetic attention, causing them to attempt to shut them down and divert the attention, that they so desperately crave, back unto themselves by spouting overgeneralising reductionist rubbish such as "everyone goes through that" or "oh yeah? Well, something even worse happened to me". Ironically, such drivel drools out the same gorming mouths of 'people' who will cry of the importance of their own well-being difficulties and expect everyone to treat them with kindness, despite their own perfect displays of mindboggling stupidity when refusing to adopt the fundamental person-centred approach to appreciate the true giants others face. Observing hypocritical behaviour of friends when you are vulnerable is a great way of discovering any toxicity permeating your friendship. For example, should one observe that they contradict their sacred values by proceeding to be blissfully judgemental just after condemning judgemental behaviour, hypothetically speaking, then one will have observed the unauthentic forms of their supposedly authentic friends. Authentic friendships should be empathetic, non-judgemental, and genuine circles of trust whereby real friends feel comfortable opening up about their personal struggles, devoid of the fear of judgement.

Sad to say, this lack of emotional and perhaps even general intelligence is not so uncommon among even the most mature of Westerners. Often incapable of 'achieving' mere communication with people with a different political perspective to their own precious little opinions, Westerners are among the most tragically unintelligent creatures to ever live.

The Wisdom of the Unauthentic Friend

For both the purposes of entertainment and further highlighting how an unauthentic friend might destructively disregard the importance of the well-being of others, below, is a written text satirising what an unauthentic friend might say and think:

> *"Mental health issues? I can help. I'm the therapist of my friend group. Stefan was once moaning to me that his ex was preventing him from seeing his only child (drama queen), so I cured his depression by responding that my personal issues were way worse than that so he should just stop feeling sorry for himself, it's pathetic. He's not complained to me since, so he's clearly happy now.*

Yeah, I got fired from 10/20 min-wage jobs, so? I have a trustfund! I once held an apprenticeship for 6 months. My failure manager friends made fun of me for earning £4.50ph, but I said at least one of us has a future. So, after getting fired, I poured myself 10 pints and asked my gf what was next. She's an assistant to the manager at Pizza Hut and gets FREE PIZZA! Do my cocky mates get free pizza? Hell no, all they get is independent financial security and self-respect which is boooring! Expertly, she told me to get new friends. I tried, but nobody in Dursley was free at the time, shithole anyway. Meanwhile, as soon as I saw my mates next, I called them all ugly, they usually don't say anything back because they 'feel bad for me' or something, but this time Karl called me fat. The fucking audacity! How dare that ugly cunt insult me for the way I look, how can I help that, by dieting? Give me a break, diets are for insecure women. I'm not even fat anyway, I only weigh the same as 25 stones.

Finally, when you see a guy rocking a pair of tatty, beer-stained jeans worn with a baggy flannel shirt from NEXT, recognise that that is elite style. I should know, my sister is doing BA Fashion at London Met. Also, to all the sheep wearing GUCCI, fuck you, and no, I'm not just saying that because I can't afford it; I'm 30, I could bully my Mum into getting luxury designer for me if I wanted to.

Some people say I should wear deodorant, but why? I already shower once a month. I'm a slayer, born to slay. Anyone that judges another is probably autistic, so fuck them. Being in the same room as me should be considered an honour... a big room... with a lot of air-con."

Conclusively, the unauthentic friend's malicious behaviour may actually be resultant of their own low self-esteem, meaning that their cruelty is probably just a projection of their own personal insecurities. A kind person might see them as a lost soul longing for the attention deprived of them by their father, possibly.

Therefore, perhaps if one was to ask them what is wrong, should they see such behaviour, then their unauthenticity may be cured. Overall, this newly contagious compassion is likely to improve the stability of the friendship group.

The Need for Independence and Selfhood

If one is suffering the misfortune of having unauthentic friends and they do not wish to change them, then they should resort to cutting them off. Unauthentic people will look to halt one's personal development out of jealousy, to both unintentionally and intentionally embarrass them in public, and to eat away at one's own authenticity. A departing friend owes no one an explanation. So, if other people are making you feel miserable, for any reason, then they should remove them from your life, in order to improve it. Only the self knows what sort of crowd they fit into, so if they think their current crowd is 'below' them, that is OK to recognise, they should just act on it rather than hurting others or worse, themself. However, once one wishes to enter into a new friendship, then they must use what they have learnt to pick authentic friends.

It is critical that one develops social connections, just as it is critical that one develops self-security and independence, so as to evade relying on others to feel alive and purposed. It is imperative to the self's mental health that they create a sense of individual direction and meaning, an essence, which is entirely personal and uninfluenced by social factors. However, before one can think existentially, they must shamelessly put themselves before others, even their friends and family. It is human nature to put oneself first, this is why so many others do it, and by acknowledging this, one can achieve the personal resilience that allows them to become a self. Through independence, one will overcome many social factors that cause them despair. For example, they will no longer experience a fear of missing out (FOMO) as they are indifferent to the affairs of others, and become highly resistant to criticism as they do not care what others think of them, except for, say, very close family members who can help them be a better self. Once a self, one can bask in the eternal glory of selfhood, feeling no impulse to conform to the will of external influences. For example, a self will be immune to being politically radicalised, being peer pressured into drug abuse, or being socialised into gang crime by unauthentic friends. Instead, the authentic self will forever be true to themselves, whilst they remain in selfhood. However, some methods of influence are less obviously harmful, thus, they can still attract a self back down into despair. A good example of this type of guile is made apparent through unhealthy subcultural lifestyles, like 'dark academia'. The aesthetic and literature within Dark academia is clearly appealing and might attract some selves. Unfortunately, those who eventually base their lifestyles on such disturbing subcultures hold a harmful tendency to adopt unhealthy conditions romanticised across the subculture, like insomnia and caffeine addiction. In extreme cases, people even self-diagnose themselves with mental illnesses, aimlessly rebel against those close to them, and inflict self-harm, all in the name of a sort of subcultural assimilation. Convincingly, unhealthy life choices can worm their way into otherwise secure people's lives through a hefty influence of their peers.

Forgive the cliché, but friends can be dangerous, so pick them wisely; a man stuck in inauthentic friendship circles is lonelier than a man that just has himself.

Chapter Eighteen: Abuse

Abuse in the West

As compared to the rest of the world, abuse across the West seems to be more commonly psychological than physical, although victims can still be abused in both ways and more. To understand why this is, one should look at the contrast between protection against abuse in Western and other cultures. For example, the UK outlaws "physical or sexual abuse", "violent or threatening behaviour", "controlling or coercive behaviour", "economic abuse", and "psychological, emotional or other abuse" in the Domestic Abuse Act 2021. On the other hand, in Algeria, there are no laws against domestic violence, thus, it is not even considered to be abusive. Obviously, this does not mean that domestic abuse never occurs in the West, but it does indicate that it generally occurs less in the West than it does outside. Moreover, the vagueness of the UK's legislative protection against domestic emotional abuse persuades abusers to think that they can evade punishment for their crimes, for which aggravating factors of evidence will be more abstract and difficult for investigators to identify, unlike the observable evidence for physical abuse.

Of course, forms of abuse are not just limited to physical or psychological, but they all have negative psychological effects on victims. For example, victims of discriminatory, financial, and physical abuse alike might all subsequently feel an angst when they find themselves in a related scenario once again. This is because being abused will lower a victim's self-image and make them feel vulnerable.

Behaviourism and Learned Helplessness

'Learned helplessness' is the behaviourist theory that claims a series of unpleasant experiences will socialise a person into maintaining a passive attitude when experiencing unpleasant events in the future. To elaborate, a victim of child abuse might not resist being raped in their adults years as they have learned that attempting to influence the situations around them is futile and that they are helpless. This feeling of passive acceptance of being subjected to terrible experiences is a common cause for clinical depression and other mood disorders, according to behaviourists.

Someone who has a learned helplessness is also known by some anti-academics to be suffering from 'victim mentality'. Unfortunately, cruel and unempathetic labels, such as that, only serve to further demoralise and alienate victims of abuse, meaning that they are also less likely to report any others cases of abuse for fear of being stitched with another insulting label, such as being an attention seeker.

To learn a state of helplessness is also to commit a logical fallacy. Specifically, to feel helplessness in every situation where resistance is required to overcome it is to exaggerate the impact and overgeneralise the range of one's own helplessness. Naturally, a person who attributes a group of negative situations with a fundamental outcome is not thinking rationally, and when this outcome is negative, they are also not thinking healthily. Instead, they should analyse the problem and actively look for solutions until they solve said problem. According to behaviourists, this cure is found when a person's self-efficacy is raised so that they can understand that, through their own actions, they can make a difference.

The concept of learned helplessness might explain why so many survivors of sexual abuse took so long to speak out against their abusers. Aside from its more recent reliability limitations, the #MetToo movement, for instance, saw cases of sexual harassment against former film producer Harvey Weinstein dating back to the 1970s brought into the public eye as more than eighty women collectively came forward with their individual stories. See, before anyone dared to accuse Weinstein, these women may have learned a sense of helplessness due to the gender inequality and misogyny that was permeating Hollywood at the time, but once one voice was heard then the others soon followed as the brave women broke the passivity to sexual misconduct as a team.

Similarly, victims of domestic violence are often forced to feel helpless as their abusers make them feel entrapped, whilst also gaslighting them by denying that they are a victim of any form of abusive behaviour. Thankfully, some women are gifted with the insurmountable bravery required to free themselves from the shackles of such a horrible household. For example, Jen Dymond, a small business owner based in the East Midlands, has been dubbed "Wonder Woman" for her demonstration of masterful selflessness, solicitude, and valour by how she refused to be beaten by her physically and emotionally abusive ex-husband, even managing to relocate herself and her children, Ashley and Rosie, from Devon to Derbyshire, allowing them both to lead fulfilling and important lives. By recognising her own independent ability to take action, she was able to literally save lives. However, Dymond is privileged with a steady head and a stout heart, thus, one cannot claim that every victim should just take control. The reality is that some people, as tragic as it is, will dwell in an abusive household for the rest of the life, and through their passivity, they will subject their children to inadequate socialisation, a risk of being abused, and a further risk of becoming an abuser. Conclusively, one can only stand up and be counted in order to survive.

Everyone is an agent of their own life, so goes the truth of the existential thinker. Granted, victims of abuse do not choose to be abused, but for as long as they bear the gift of free-will, they can change their life for the better and overcome anything. People must remember that they are in control if they wish to change their destiny.

Senior Vulnerability: Financial Abuse and Neglect

Since the Thatcher administration, Britain's health and social care sector has undergone a gradual process of privatisation. Today, the vast majority of residential and domiciliary care providers are private companies, as opposed to being state-run like the majority of said services before Margaret Thatcher's glorious rule. As health and social care services as now mostly private, they are not subject to governmental responsibility and are only motivated by profit in a free market. Due to this, contemporary left-wing and centrist social critics have suggested that capitalism has contributed to the disregard for the welfare of the elderly. For example, socialists suggest that private companies extort the wealthy elderly, who do not try to negotiate for either a lack of motivation or cognitive impairment, and will continue to do so for as long as they are allowed to charge whatever fees they like. Additionally, these critics advocate that residential homes should be exclusively run by the NHS because public health would use skilled negotiators to beat down any external costs, thus preventing a (borderline) abusive sense of financial predatory behaviour. Across Britain, social care services are largely built for profit and they prey on the frail elderly who are made vulnerable by the lack of economic support and dementia awareness in society. Residential homes often fail to meet the needs of their residents, though this failure cannot really be blamed on the home managers because these people are instructed to manage a budget more than they are to develop and maintain an inclusive environment with core values promoting the importance of best interests, equity, and the person-centred approach for their residents. Despite what the Health and Social Care Act 2012 might say, humanistic values are few and far between across the sector and there is little evidence to suggest any progressive growth consequent of the legislation. However, a tiny minority of private care companies do attempt to incorporate humanistic ideals into their policies and procedures. For example, some service providers have taken it upon themselves to integrate Italian physician Maria Montessori's philosophy of education into adult care practices by encouraging residents with disabilities to engage in educational activities that stimulate their interests to regain their lost abilities in a non-judgemental environment. For example, a person who has lost the ability the feed themselves due to arthritis might be given a special set of cutlery that they are more comfortable with in order to reactivate their independence, thus, boosting their self-esteem. Moreover, some legislative protection in the UK does hold theoretically progressive concepts that promote and protect an elderly person's right to a high quality of life via the adoption of an equitable approach. The Mental Capacity Act 2005, particularly, protects elderly people living with dementia by supplying them with an advocate who, should the individual with dementia be professionally deemed to have an impaired capacity to make informed decisions, ensures that their preferences are respected by their service providers. DOLS (deprivation of liberty safeguards), an amendment to the same legislation, fortifies the protection of the same individuals by incrimination the action of preventing an individual with an 'impaired capacity' a freedom to choose, even if that said choice might pose a hazardous risk to their health in the opinion of any social worker. For example, should a client wish to walk to the bathroom unaided, despite their usual dependence on a Zimmer frame, the care workers should allow them to proceed, provided that the client is able to make informed decisions. Therefore, even if care workers have tried to persuade the client to make a more informed decision, the client's final decision will always be respected regardless of what it is. Otherwise, to impede on their freedom is deemed to be a 'deprivation of [their] liberty' and is illegal. Naturally, this has the potential to create confusion for care workers when balancing the client's 'best interests' with their individual liberty, but the Care Act 2014 thankfully eases the pressure on care staff by stating that it is the sole responsibility of the service provider to work with practitioners and clients alike to establish a person-centred care plan founded upon the client's mental capacity, needs, and preferences, meaning that care staff should be fully informed and supported in understanding all clients' capacity to make decisions without threatening their dignity, risking neglecting them and their rights, or endangering them in any way.

Unfortunately, despite the limited progression made within residential facilities, elderly people are still neglected in most other areas of life. For example, many elderly people are not offered protection against online scammer artists, but when they do fall victim to fraud, they are stigmatised as careless and stupid. Until British authorities decide to take action against their own passivity towards the vulnerability of the forgotten elderly, then they can never claim that their society is equitable or inclusive. Just think, advertising free, optional courses aimed at educating elderly people about the dangers of the internet and how to conduct a more vigilant etiquette online, say, on the radio, would be so tedious a task that one could barely call it work. Yet, the government's inaction speaks volumes as it only sees that they actively neglect their own people.

Psychoanalysis

Josef Breuer, a psychiatrist who is created with having developed the 'talking cure', famously used psychotherapy to treat Bertha Pappenheim (known by the pseudonym 'Anna O'), one of his patients, by simply letting her talk about her symptoms in order to make her unconscious, repressed, traumatic memories conscious, thus, causing her symptoms to reduce. Breuer's protégé, Sigmund Freud, would then be inspired by his mentor's 'talk therapy' and would use what he had witnessed to found both a new psychotherapeutic technique in 'free association', whereby patients could make their unconscious cognitions conscious by saying what immediately came to mind in relation to a certain topic, and a new approach to psychology, psychoanalysis.

In its early years, psychoanalysis proved to be a controversial and divisive psychological theory, mostly because of two Freudian theories:
1. The id, ego, and superego.
2. The psychoanalytical sexual drive theory.

With his concept of the id, ego, and superego, Freud surprisingly proposed that everyone's conscious decisions are really dictated by unconscious influences, hence, expressing his view that free will is an illusion. Also, with his theory of psychosexual development, Freud audaciously proposed that five psychosexual stages (oral, anal, phallic, latency, and genital) formed the structure of one's id, which is a major Freudian component of human personality encompassing one's basic instincts.

Regardless of what one may think of these theories, Freud's brilliance remains undeniable; his work on psychoanalysis has left him to be arguably the most influential psychologist of all time. Specifically, through psychoanalysis, Freud conceived many more theories of psychodynamics which all held the fundamental belief that human personality is largely shaped by early life experiences and that mental health issues arise when one represses, rather than accepts or acts on, any trauma from their past, thus, also causing their unconscious personality factors to be out of balance. For example, should a person's traumatic memory mean that their superego dominates their personality, they will generally be submissive to others in dangerous scenarios, something that will probably lower their self-image and depress them. Plainly, through the psychodynamic approach, one could speculate as to explain the behaviour of victims of abuse and, to a further extent, even the behaviour of their abusers too.

Someone who was sexually abused as a child may repress their traumatic memories, become stuck on a particular psychosexual stage, and develop mental health issues consequent of an imbalance between their id, ego, and superego. Specifically, a victim of child sex abuse might develop a psychotic disorder, such as schizophrenia, that increases their levels of paranoia around other people. Similarly, a victim of child sex abuse may proceed to develop a paedophilic personality themselves, as they may have become extremely infatuated with their abuser, thus, deviating their views of such relations from what is lawfully accepted well into their later life.

Whatever one's views may be, if a victim of abuse is to become a survivor, then their story must be heard.

Chapter Nineteen: Virtue

What is Virtue?

Virtue is defined as a moral trait whereby a virtuous character will have high ethical standards, although the actual morality of these standards remain subject to controversy. Unsurprisingly, there is debate as to what constitutes one having 'good morals' or a 'virtuous character'. Some say that, in order to be virtuous, people's behaviours should conform to a clear set of rules, in the form of objective moral values, that establish the duality between good and evil. This ethical theory is called deontology and is mostly related to Immanuel Kant, a German philosopher who expressed that it is fundamentally good to be polite to others, just as it is bad to lie to them, irrespective of the outcome. Deontology runs counter to the teleological theory of consequentialism, which states that actions producing good outcomes, such as happiness, are fundamentally good. Niccolò Machiavelli, an Italian diplomat who lived during the Renaissance period, infamously claimed that the 'ends justify the means', a radically consequentialist opinion. For example, in his most popular and divisive work, 'The Prince', Machiavelli reiterates that a good-natured political candidate should do whatever they can, including hurting the lives of others, to achieve political power, where they can ultimately do good. Whilst Machiavelli is not representative of all consequentialist thinkers, such as the utilitarian Jeremy Bentham, he certainly represents the practical dangers of consequential thinking, therefore, at the risk of sounding morally biased, deontological thinkers should be regarded as more virtuous than their consequentialist counterparts.

Like consequentialism, deontology is targeted by critics for suffering from theoretical limitations. For example, Kant is criticised for assuming the existence of objective moral values on the basis of little to no physical evidence. Whilst this may seem like a valid criticism to the common man, objective moral values are inherently immaterial, thus they can only be theoretically studied. Kierkegaard, for example, offers a theoretical argument for their existence as they are fundamentally created by the self who has striven for selfhood by following a moral philosophy individually suited to them and, "you guessed it", God (try not to cry, this is not another argument for God's existence).

Morality is a topic for metaphysics; to question the physical existence of morality is to defy logic. Would one look to the skies and claim that God is not real as they cannot see Him? Objective moral values are transcendent of the naturalistic world, yet they are also real. To understand this, one need only look to their own behaviours and ask oneself what motivates them to behave. In doing so, one will, hopefully, realise that they behave in ways that are consist with their own moral code. Where does the code come from, though? Ultimately, one's morality is individually constructed. Of course, it can be socially influenced to change, but it will always be created and acted on by the self to provide them with their own sense of virtue. Conclusively, moral codes must be real because people are directed by them, yet there are also immaterial and cannot be measured, causing anger, controversy, and subjectivity which condemn people into nihilism and stupidity.

So, if objective moral values exist, but are paradoxically individually constructed, then how can virtuous people exist? Humanists answer this quite nicely. They say that, rather than by following specific philosophy, if one's moral paradigm inspires them to act with integrity in accordance with a moral philosophy that solicitously respects the culture, freedom, and welfare of other people, then one can be regarded as virtuous. On the topic of humanism, a belief that seemingly founds the basis for humanistic thinking is that humans are fundamentally good creatures. Of course, humans can still be bad people, but humanists explain this by claiming that people are socialised into adopting evil mindsets. Just something to think about…

Traditionally 'Virtuous' People

Identifying virtuous people has historically been proven to be difficult, so, to evade the complexity of adopting a more person-centred analysis of somebody's individual values, some people simply look to people's jobs to account for their morality. For instance, it is a physician's job role to help and cure patients, therefore, physicians are regarded as virtuous people. However, not all physician's follow codes of practice that can consistently be deemed virtuous. To specify, doctors advocating the use of Electroconvulsive Therapy (ECT), a neurological treatment for psychosis whereby a seizure is induced in a patient via an electrical current to their brain, do so without understanding the holistic cause of its respective effect, or more specifically why it may (and may not) work. Additionally, ECT was originally used as a sadistic psychological laboratory experiment until some researchers found instances that it had suppressed a few subjects' schizophrenic symptoms, despite the trauma resulting in side effects such as memory loss, nausea, and other long-term cognitive issues, and a practical guarantee that the subject would relapse. Today, due to obvious ethical concerns, it is used as a last resort should a patient fail to response positively to psychotherapy or medication, and consent is gained before one is administered to the treatment. However, medical regulations see that Doctors can easily manipulate patients into undergoing therapy who do not demonstrate the capacity to make an informed decision, not due to their individual cognitive ability, but as they are not fully informed. Unfortunately, this is something that one seems to be able to generalise as to account for the way Western healthcare is underpinned by the anti-holistic biomedical model of health. Clearly, ECT is incredibly dangerous because of the risk-assessment negligence that its mere existence poses; doctors do not understand the hazards ECT can causes to human health, therefore not a soul can be allowed to act surprised when patients are harmed. Overall, Doctors want to help their patients, but they do so at the further risk of the patient's health, thus, one cannot measure someone's virtuous nature through analysis of any organisation that said person is a member of, such as their profession.

Objective, but not Absolute, Moral Values

Whilst people create their own objective moral values and live in accordance with them based on their own sense of self, other people are bound to live by moralities that will be utterly inconsistent with that of the former's, as individual senses of self are very different to one another. To be optimistic, all this should mean is that, whilst one's morality objectively exists (with its existence unable to be subjectively questioned), moral values are not absolute, so people will naturally function based on their own moral paradigm. Tragically, however, Westerners feel entitled enough to recklessly judge other people for their own truths, thus, they will condemn behaviours that they disagree with.

Tribalism, a culture so evidently imperative to the West of today, only serves to aggravate the detrimental consequences of harsh interpersonal judgement. For instance, a group of radical leftists unified by their shared values and norms, rather than an individual centrist, will socially isolate those with more right-wing views than their own as they have been radicalised to a level of extremism that renders them intolerant of other people's beliefs, irrespective of any of their individual or cultural difference that determines that they will develop different moral paradigms that are correctly tailored to them as a self. This irrational but popular sense of social exclusion always hurt a person's self-image for human beings are naturally social creatures. Obviously, with a lower self-image comes mood disorders, like manic depression, that will distort and interfere with a person's ability to function.

The plain and simple truth about virtue, despite all of its apparent contradictions and its theoretical complexities, is that it is a fundamental aspect of the human character. Without virtue, or virtuous integrity, people will lose what makes them human.

Chapter Twenty: Conclusion

An Initial Summary

To neatly recap on the messages of the individual chapters, their explanations on how their topic stimulates the development of mental health issues are summarised below:

Chapter 2. Technology:
    a. Technological developments are vast.
    b. Human authenticity is being replaced with technological imitations.
    c. Soon, empathy will be rendered obsolete by a paradox of illogical logic.

Chapter 3. Icons:
    a. People look up to their icons.
    b. Icons are superficial and inauthentic.
    c. People who dream of living the iconic lifestyle will only live a nightmare in practice.

Chapter 4.   Entertainment:
   a.   The modern entertainment industry is a by-product of the West, thus, it portrays characters and narratives that are consistent with its own social norms.
   b.   Some social groups are insufficiently represented in film and TV.
   c.   However, what constitutes sufficient representation is complicated and the demand for it is misplaced.

Chapter 5.   Mass Media:
   a.   Mass media outlets are forever biased and ridden with hidden agendas.
   b.   People are radicalised into extremism by the media.
   c.   The targets of extremism will be severely emotionally affected.

Chapter 6.   Social Media:
   a.   Social media is very poorly regulated.
   b.   People are abused on social media so often that it is now a form of culture.
   c.   In order to prioritise their mental health, people should stay away from social media.

Chapter 7.   Materialism:
   a.   The West's socioeconomic structure is capitalistic, thus, it eternalises materialism.

  b. Materialism encourages cutthroat, selfish, and shallow attitudes and behaviour.
  c. People who are without much material wealth are usually also without a strong self-esteem.

Chapter 8. Socialisation:
  a. The family and the education system both function to teach children the shared norms and values of society.
  b. Dysfunctional families might socialise children into deviance; the anti-intellectual nature of academia ensures that children conform to an exclusively 'correct' way of thinking.
  c. Children learn to socially ostracise deviant people.

Chapter 9. Occupation:
  a. People will usually work at a similar hierarchal level to their parents.
  b. Social mobility is very rare.
  c. People who work in jobs that they feel no personal relationship with are bound to despair and dissociate from reality.

Chapter 10. Liberty:
  a. The West houses highly liberal societies.
  b. The West is excessively liberal; Westerns are cited as solely responsible for their own life outcomes.

    c.   People cannot accept their own failures and fall into spirals of depression and anxiety.

Chapter 11.   Social Order:
    a.   Western societies are built to function in highly specific ways.
    b.   The social order of society functions to oppress some of its citizens.
    c.   The oppressed citizens are inclined to commit suicide.

Chapter 12.   Social Divisions:
    a.   When people think of globalisation, they actually think of Westernisation.
    b.   Humans beings are fragile yet ruthless creatures. If they are segregated, they will fight, conform to tribalism, weaponise ideology, and disregard individual differences in favour of a militant sense of unity.
    c.   Social divisions are the antithesis to a truly inclusive society as they cater for the many but not the few.

Chapter 13.   Criminal Justice:
    a.   Criminals are abandoned by a society that either refuses, or simply cannot rehabilitate them.
    b.   Most criminals are ostracised in the same culture that pushed them into crime.
    c.   If the West is to change this, then it must alter its shared norms and values.

Chapter 14. Healthcare:
    a. It is impossible to prove the existence of mental illnesses, at least via the adoption of quantitative research methods.
    b. Social deviance is medicalised and illnesses are socially constructed.
    c. People diagnosed with illnesses are made to feel like nuisances and are ostracised from society.

Chapter 15. Individuality – Part One:
    a. Nobody understands other people, but they can get close if they try.
    b. Society renders people judgemental and ingenuine, thus, they neglect the importance of empathy.
    c. In order to empathise with others and appreciate the complexities of the human subjective experience, one must take a person-centred approach.

Chapter 16. Individuality – Part Two:
    a. Nobody understands themselves, but they can get close if they try.
    b. Self-reflection is key to avoiding despair and entering into selfhood.
    c. If you omit the individual, your view of life is incredibly limited.

Chapter 17. Friendship:

       a.   Toxic friendships are inauthentic and depressing.
       b.   Losers want to see others lose, just as winners want to see winners win.
       c.   Surround yourself with winners in order to win.

Chapter 18.   Abuse:
       a.   Victims of abuse are haunted by their past.
       b.   Victims of abuse learn a passive feeling of helplessness.
       c.   In order to overcome their helplessness, survivors must unlock their repressed traumatic memories, awaken their unconscious thoughts, then begin thinking rationally.

Chapter 19.   Virtue:
       a.   Deontology is morality superior to consequentialism.
       b.   When one believes that the ends justify the means, there is not much that they will not do.
       c.   The West perpetuates Machiavellianism; it greatly threatens the well-being of its own citizenry.

A Final Word

What is life? Whilst Kierkegaard proposed three modes of existence: the aesthetic, ethical, or the religious, true to his character, Dostoevsky was considerably more blunt. With tears of sorrow, the Russian novelist conceded that humans are all too flawed to live perfectly, and no social uprising or scientific revolution will save them from the truth; the truth that to live is to suffer.

Alas, one rule has helped this writer, who once despaired, to navigate the Western sadness:

"Do not question whether you are the son that your father would be proud of. Ask yourself, are you the man you want your son to be?"

Printed in Great Britain
by Amazon